A PATRIOT'S CALL
TO ACTION

A PATRIOT'S CALL TO ACTION

Resisting Progressive Tyranny & Restoring Constitutional Order

Jim Delaney

To order additional copies of this book, contact:
Xlibris
1-888-795-4274
www.Xlibris.com
Orders@Xlibris.com
599549

Contents

"A nation of well-informed men who have been taught to know and prize the rights which God has given them cannot be enslaved. It is in the region of ignorance that tyranny begins." Benjamin Franklin

ACKNOWLEDGMENTS

I want to especially thank Rick Montes, NYS Tenth Amendment Center, for his encouragement and suggestions, without which this book would not have been attempted.

I would also like to acknowledge scholars like W. Cleon Skousen, David Barton, Kevin Gutzman, Robert Natelson, Thomas Woods, Donald Livingston, Brion McClanahan, John Remington Graham, and so many others for their instructive publications which have added so much to my understanding of and appreciation for the Constitution.

Thanks also to my friends, John Mickles and John Sotack, without whose computer savvy I could not have pulled this off. And for generously underwriting this project, my special thanks to nephew Todd Ryan Delaney.

Finally, I want to extend my heartfelt gratitude to all those nameless patriots in the trenches out there who, in the spirit of our Founders, have unselfishly committed so much energy, talent and passion to the daunting effort of restoring constitutional order in these United States of America. Many of you may not know it now, but your unwavering devotion to our founding principles has been the only thing standing between tyranny and liberty in America. Never surrender!

Vox populi, vox Dei

PREFACE

For Progressives to fundamentally transform these United States of America into yet another failed utopian state requires that our Constitution be reduced to irrelevance and that our electorate remains befuddled, polarized and misled. Toward that end, and often with Republican complicity, Progressives have been nothing short of masterful.

Committed to stemming the Progressive assault on our way of life and to protect what remains of our tattered Republic, in my small way I decided to try to make a difference. I began to post articles on every receptive blog site I could find, regularly submit editorials to my local newspapers, and to become more actively engaged in the Tea Party Movement.

After nearly five years of researching and active engagement, I began to understand that We the People have been essentially alienated by the political elites, so many of whom have abandoned our founders' wisdom and commonsense, brashly ignored the lessons of history, and, in the process, undermined the foundations of our Constitution. In truth, voicing my concerns to my "representatives" had been reduced to a frustrating exercise in futility.

Infested with career elites at all levels of government who, by in large, are no longer guided by our highest ideals as a constitutional republic, it is clear that our focus must now be on educating our fellow citizens, uniting patriots in order to forge a unified action plan for effective resistance, and convincing our State leadership to invoke the 10th Amendment to nullify federal excesses and lawlessness, failing which our unalienable right to "dissolve the political bands which have connected" us may be our only salvation.

Clearly, the solution to our menacing economic and political problems lies not on luck and hope, or a delusional belief that all will somehow work out for the best without our personal engagement, but in our unshakeable reliance upon and faithfulness to both the original meaning of the Constitution and our Christian precepts.

My articles in this book are intended to be introductory and instructional. Bite-sized in length, each article is intended to provoke discussion, to stimulate further exploration of our founding principles, and to urge readers to fearlessly re-commit themselves to preserving, protecting and defending the Constitution of the United States from all enemies, both foreign AND domestic.

[1] RESISTING TYRANNY

Is Patriotism Alone Enough?

Of late, there's been much *talk* on conservative blogs about uniting and moving forward with more energy and effectiveness. While I am heartened by that sentiment, I am mindful that actions always speak louder than words.

We can do what we can to organize locally, as many of us have done, and to actively participate in the local political party machine to effect change from within, as some of us have also done, but that is simply NOT enough.

The major parties are powerful and influential precisely because they are well-coordinated and well-organized both locally and nationally. Thus, patriotic organizations' deliberately or unwittingly restricting themselves to localized activity alone is inadequate.

The truth is we need to be organized locally, regionally and nationally. Otherwise, we will be less than credible or effective, membership and participation will continue to dissipate, and the country will further careen into oblivion.

If patriotic organizations remain splintered and parochial, we are doomed, as is our country. It's time for patriots to get very, VERY serious and much more activist. Learn from the Left!

Obviously, someone of national renown needs to lead the charge by encouraging local and regional alliances, and by promoting the timely convening of a representative "national convention of patriots" which would represent those local/regional alliances, this in order to fashion a genuinely national ACTION AGENDA to take back our country. Who knows, such a convening might even result in the birth of a formidable political party which will attract adherents from both the left and the right--well, from the right anyway.

Among others, I would urge LTC Allen West, Sen. Mike Lee, former Senator Coburn and/or Sarah Palin to lead this charge. I can only hope they are reading this. But, assuming they aren't, I emailed them a copy of this article.

A re-energized national Tea Party movement comprised of millions of Tea Partiers and other patriots from all over the country coalescing around one activist agenda would seriously threaten the entrenched establishment and would, I think, compel the GOP to either adopt a convincing first-principles agenda going forward or face the certainty of irrelevance and impotence.

Being organized and well-coordinated on both a local and national level would most certainly stem the Progressive tide and would preclude the contemplation of secession or rebellion. Splintered, however, the TP and other patriotic entities will remain a nearly useless therapeutic matrix of venting platforms--a lot of sound and fury of precious little consequence.

Faithfully grassroots in orientation, but national in scope, patriots' clout would be greatly enhanced. Being thoroughly grassroots, thereby honoring the maxim that all politics is local, our ground game alone could more easily flip both State and DC elective offices.

As for a "national convention of patriots", think of such a historical convening as the 21st century equivalent of the 18th century pre-revolution Committees of Correspondence. Tell me that didn't make a gargantuan difference in America's destiny! Let history and the basics of "community organizing", the latter which makes the Leftist radicals so powerful in spite of their vacuous and destructive agenda, be our guide.

No more inconsequential pontificating, whining, woe-is-me, venting to the choir, and increasingly hollow TP rallies to the exclusion of a more activist regional and nationalist agenda. Much MUCH more is needed if we are to save what little remains of this Republic. Activism works!

On the local level, let each of us begin in earnest the unifying process. And let's make it all come together as though our lives and the lives of our children depended upon it—because they do!

A CALL TO CONVENTION

(Draft Appeal/Invitation to Patriotic Organization Leaders in your Area)

ACTIVISM: the doctrine or practice of _vigorous_ action or *involvement* as a means of achieving political or other goals, sometimes by demonstrations, protests, sit-ins, etc.

Dear Patriots,

Our Republic is in serious political and economic peril.

Is it too late to reverse our nation's slide into darkness? (If we believe it is too late, then the path before us is clear: appease, adapt and surrender.)

Over the next four years, what remains of our Constitutional Republic might well be lost to us and our progeny forever. (On a very personal level, we must each honestly gauge how compelling and motivating that awful possibility may be.)

In the face of a relentless and ruthless authoritarian assaults on our freedoms and way of life, what are we to do? What are we WILLING to do? Placidly accommodate those dark forces or more effectively and vigorously resist?

Is it time for concerted ACTION to more effectively repel the multitude of assaults upon our lives, liberties and property? (Or are we content to merely venting our frustrations to fellow patriots?)

What specific actions are needed? In unity and with the foundational constitutional principles as our guide, what actions are we ALL willing to fearlessly act upon? Which of those actions might be most effective?

Bottom line: for most of us, it IS time to A-C-T with determination, discipline, clarity of purpose and in unbreakable unity. (If patriots remain disunited, parochial, fractious and uncoordinated, then the authoritarians will easily prevail.)

PROPOSAL

PRE-CONVENTION MEETING: Representatives/Organizers are asked to meet_sometime before_____20__ to discuss and draft an action plan/agenda. (Each is also urged to identify and to encourage participation in this pre-convention meeting of other patriotic representatives/organizers in their respective areas.) Perhaps a Saturday or Sunday might be most convenient.

The purpose of this pre-convention meeting is to develop a meaningful, activist grassroots action plan/agenda aimed at more effectively resisting federal (and state) overreach.

At this pre-convention meeting, Organizers will decide upon either a temporary or permanent Convener from among the participating Representatives/Organizers. (How that is to be handled can be decided at the pre-convention meeting.)

DEVELOPING A FINAL DRAFT ACTION PLAN/AGENDA: Reps/Organizers will promptly share the pre-convention draft action plan/agenda with their respective members and elicit their timely suggestions/feedback. The aim is to develop more effective, vigorous action(s) in which members would be willing to actively participate or would be willing to substantively support. Simultaneously, members should be asked to recommend a workable meeting date/time, location for a General Convention of Patriots in _____20__.)

In a timely fashion, each Rep/Organizer will briefly summarize all actions proposed by their respective members and share same with fellow Reps/Organizers via email for their review. The Convener will prepare a list of all suggested actions and email same to all fellow Reps/Organizers for their information and for on-forwarding to their respective members for their review as well.

CONVENTION OF PATRIOTS: based upon all feedback and per online discussion with fellow Reps/Organizers, a date/time/location for a general "Convention of Patriots" to review and adopt an action plan will be finalized. The date/place/location of Convention will to immediately relayed to members through their respective Reps/Organizers. Each Rep/

Organizer will gauge members' commitment to attend and will relay that count to fellow Reps/Organizers and to the Convener, this to ensure an appropriate meeting venue is arranged.

PROPOSED TIMELINE

CONVENTION OF PATRIOTS: PROPOSED TIMELINE (in WEEKS)										
Event	1	2	3	4	5	6	7	8	9	10
Pre-Convention Meeting Prep	■									
Pre-Convention Meeting		■								
Reps/Organizers collect input from respective members re action plan suggestions and general convention date/time/place			■							
Reps/Organizers forward member feedback re action plan items & suggested convention meeting date/time/location to Convener for summarizing and distribution to Fellow Organizers					■					
Convener will arrange and confirm agreed upon time/location for general Convention, and, in turn, Reps/Organizers will relay that information to their members							■			
General "Convention of Patriots"								■		
Next Steps . . .									■	■

NUNC AUT NUNQUAM
(Now or never)

Notes: Someone in your area must take the initiative to put this plan into action. To arrange appropriate accommodation for a Convention of Patriots, conveners may need to request donations from patriot group Reps/Organizers and, in turn, their respective members and supporters.

Nitwits, Pollyannas and Marxists

It's well past time to see things as they really are, and not the way we'd like to see them.

It's well past time to vigorously confront the mendacity and treason of Progressive propagandists and political hacks at all levels and on both sides of the aisle.

For us to continue to tolerate, appease and compromise with these shameless alien ideologues and soulless demagogues must now be regarded by patriots everywhere as dishonorable, suicidal and, thus, without any redeeming value whatsoever.

Without rehashing the litany of lies and obscurantism so unabashedly exhibited by Progressives, for the informed and clear-eyed among us it should now be painfully obvious that owing to the relentless Progressive assault on our political, cultural and economic foundations, our liberties and way of life are imperiled as never before. If we are to thwart the "fundamental transformation of the USA", the Progressive threat to our very survival must be boldly confronted head on and resisted at every turn.

The cacophony of odious scandals and the Progressives' ruthless advancement of secularism and egalitarianism now influences every facet of our society--the military, the government at all levels, our schools and churches, our moral precepts, and now the healthcare system itself. Why? Because dedicated Progressives understand that for Communism to triumph, the State must successfully undermine the family and religious faith, eliminate the people's ability to defend themselves and to control both their healthcare and the education of their children. And toward that end, the success of Progressive treachery--with the compliance of self-serving elitist enablers on the right as well--has been nothing short of spectacular.

Long ago hijacked by Socialists and outright Marxists, we must be fully mindful that the modern Democratic Party's march toward utopian tyranny is frighteningly on pace to completely wreck the most exceptional experiment in self-government the world has ever known. Sadly, however, far too many Americans have opted to sit idly by as this bone-chilling carnage is perpetrated.

But, we who are still able to see and think and to differentiate between good and evil--and now even a few malcontents on the left--understand that Socialism/Communism violates Natural Law and is, therefore, unworkable and self-destructive. The bountiful historical evidence to substantiate this historical contenton is simply too overwhelming for any rational being to seriously discount. As XM Radio's Andrew Wilkow of "Wilkow Majority" so succinctly stated recently, *the dumbest capitalist can make capitalism work, but the smartest socialist can't make socialism work.* For the hardcore leftist, however, this fundamental and unassailable historical truth is nothing more than vile racism wrapped in apostasy.

As today's telltale polls so clearly and disturbingly indicate, among us there are those who believe that all will work out for the best (the Pollyannas, disengaged and uninformed), those who have lost the ability to rationally think at all (the Nitwits), and, of course, the either willfully ignorant or dedicated Marxist Progressives who, bereft of a moral compass, remain hell-bent on blindly steering the ship of state toward certain political collapse and economic oblivion.

Though the malignant cancer of Progressivism/Marxism continues to metastasize throughout our social, economic and political fabric, and despite the growing and unsettling prospect of tyranny's triumph, it's still not too late for determined patriots to prevent this Progressive-induced catastrophe.

Yes, the old republic is in tatters, hanging precariously by a thread, and we have many more years of corrosive Progressive subversion with which to contend. In truth, Uncle Sam is near exhaustion and can't take much more before he expires and his "indivisible union" completely falls apart. Thus, only determined, principled, fearless and unified patriotic pushback can restore our exceptionalism and our way of life.

Given the chasmic ideological divide which exists in this nation today, bipartisanship and political compromise have become virtually unachievable. In this zero-sum ideological struggle, it's become crystal-clear that political compromise with Progressives will not ensure prosperity, rule of law, constitutional order or the inviolability of the American Way, but, rather, surrender and tyranny. For many patriots, therefore, compromising with Progressives is no longer viewed as a reasonable or moral course of action. Understandably, and for many chastened patriots today, compromising with or accommodating Progressives has become synonymous with appeasement and a green light for national suicide. And, for the most part, that's precisely what appeasement has wrought.

Drawing on our Founders' wisdom, I believe we should each carefully and honestly weigh the domestic ideological challenges besetting us, and be fully prepared for what may likely be the Republic's political disintegration and economic ruin. To ameliorate the effects of a nationwide political and economic collapse, I urge all patriots to keep all constitutional and God-given remedies on the table--civil disobedience, state nullification, secession and rebellion.

And always remember that We the People are the ultimate arbiters of what is and what is not constitutional. As guardians of the Constitution and of our Natural Rights, We the People must determine our national destiny, but also the extent of our individual liberties and of our political connections with the whole. This duty cannot be delegated to authoritarian apparatchiks whose single-minded and sinister goal is to dominate every facet of our lives--NOT to judiciously and responsibly represent our legitimate rights as citizens of a once great republic.

("Tolerance and Apathy are the last virtues of a dying society." Aristotle*)*

("When injustice becomes law, resistance becomes duty." Thomas Jefferson*)*

("A nation can survive its fools, and even the ambitious. But it cannot survive treason from within. An enemy at the gates is less formidable, for he is known and carries his banner openly. But the traitor moves amongst those within the gate freely, his sly whispers rustling through all the alleys, heard in the very halls of government itself...a murderer is less to fear. The traitor is the plague." Cicero*)*

("If the federal government should overpass the just bounds of its authority and make a tyrannical use of its powers, the people, whose creature it is, must appeal to the standard they have formed, and take such measures to redress the injury done to the Constitution as the exigency may suggest and prudence justify." Alexander Hamilton*)*

Is America's Transformation Inevitable?

When *outrageous* becomes the norm, we've already breached that much-touted tipping point and are now plunging headlong toward national suicide.

Despite the serial lawlessness, betrayal and incremental foundational self-destruction being perpetrated upon us by our political overseers, so many of us have either not noticed, not fully grasped the phenomenon, been stunned into compliance, or become inured.

Short on principled leaders and statesmen determined to faithfully defend our Constitution and absent an energetic and virtuous electorate--the very building blocks of a viable republic--an insidious and likely irreversible transformation of our way of life and governing principles is most certainly well underway. That said, one has to question if our Founders foresaw such changes and, if so, what would they have counseled?

Unlike the Articles of Confederation which established a *"perpetual* union"--and we can all see how "perpetual" that turned out to be--the Constitution's purpose was to establish a *"more* perfect union"--not perfect, but *more perfect*.

Stellar students of history, our Founders understood that no compact/contract could ever be perfect or perpetual; that all compacts, if breached, are subject to the equitable remedy of *rescission* (annulment), which, in the context of our voluntary compact of States, is equivalent to the concept of a State's *secession* (withdrawal), the converse of a State's *accession* (consent to join).

Of special significance, never once did our perceptive Founders view the "more perfect union" of States as "indivisible", a self-serving Lincolnesque invention to justify the north's invasion of the south, or that our union, with or without a clash of arms, would stand the test of time. In fact, contingent on their grudging consent to ratify the Constitution, and with nary a peep of protest from either Federalists or Anti-Federalists, Maryland, Virginia and Rhode Island, the latter which ratified the Constitution only after George Washington's election, explicitly reserved their right to *rescind/revoke* their ratification, or, in other words, withdraw from the union, if they became disenchanted with the arrangement. Thus, the Founders--framers and ratifiers alike--never believed that withdrawal from the union would be anything but a principled, entirely lawful, natural, and foreseeable development.

From the outset, and despite outrageously muddled revisionist judicial opinions, e.g. *Texas v White* (1869), and decades of revisionist indoctrination following the deliberately misnamed "civil war", this compact of States, the *united* States of America, was understood by the Founders to be strictly voluntary. And like it or not, this voluntary union remains just that--voluntary. And no amount of revisionism or political correctness can alter that foundational truth.

Like in any contractual relationship, violations occur and conditions develop which render the original contract of no further use, benefit or relevance to one or more parties to that contract. Thus, *perpetual* was never intended to convey permanence or immutability, but, like any contract, a temporariness dictated by the benefits derived from that relationship by the parties to that contract. (The Articles of Confederation is a good example of the realistic limitations of the word "perpetual" for, as we all know, the Articles of Confederation quickly outlived is usefulness and was replaced by the States and their citizens with a federal republic in 1788.)

Astute students of history, both the Framers and Ratifiers clearly understood that, over time, no man-made political system could successfully resist corruption, mutation, transformation and, yes, eventual self-destruction. In short, they understood that the historical constancy of change and mankind's need to painfully re-learn history's unpleasant lessons is as hard-wired as DNA itself.

For reasonably serious students of history, there is nothing especially profound about the foregoing observations, but in these perilous times of gargantuan national debt, a chasmic ideological divide among the electorate and its representatives, relentless violations of the Constitution at all levels of government, rampant lawlessness and habitual mendacity among our political leadership, and, yes, *crippling subversion of our political system and the country's cultural fabric from within*, dramatic systemic change is not only inevitable, but is already taking place. In short, our rapid transformation from a federal union of

States to a unitary corporatist-welfare state has been underway for some time now.

As for our *federal republic*, or what little remains of it, let's remember that a citizenry's commitment to political union at ANY price is sheer folly. If our economic, social and political systems fail to adequately safeguard our inalienable rights and our representative form of government, then our adherence to that political union is not only short-sighted, it is breathtakingly delusional and manifestly suicidal.

Going forward, I can only hope that preserving our God-given natural rights to Life, Liberty and the Pursuit of Happiness will be our primary goal. And when it becomes crystal-clear that the federal union has failed us, then from a practical standpoint our options are limited to either emigrating to other more accommodating countries or relocating to those individual States within the current union where more fertile ground for constitutional and economic order may exist.

Remember that NOT ONCE did any of the Founders in any way deny our fundamental right to secede or revolt. (Indeed, the venerable *Declaration of Independence*, was our first successful act of secession, and the American Revolution our first act of revolution.)

From the outset, our Founders soberly understood that the union's days were, indeed, numbered. In fact, most of them would have been unsurprised by the so-called "civil war", though they would have bridled at the north's lawless actions to prevent the south's secession. At a terrible price in American treasure and lives, and only by application of overwhelming military force--not virtuous adherence to founding constitutional precepts--was the north able to quash the legitimate southern secession/war for independence in 1861. And, of course, the systemic legacy of that costly Pyrrhic northern victory has been nothing less than the substantive transformation of our federal republic into something very much at odds with the political arrangement our Founders had so carefully crafted and adopted. Why Pyrrhic? Because since the conclusion of the War for Southern Independence, States have become vassals of an essentially boundless central government, something our Founders would have roundly condemned. That said, however, it appears that most of us have accepted monarchical rule so long as we are able to effectively delude ourselves into believing that this union of States is still a "republic".

To a man, our Founders would be astonished that the union today, a shattered copy of what was originally conceived, still remains at all. Thus, as said, if our best efforts fail to restore constitutional order on a national level, and if the electoral process continues to fail to restore the union as originally conceived, then the original compact among the States is, for all practical purposes, null and void, and has been null and void for some time now. Unsurprisingly, authoritarianism and, eventually, disunion are but natural consequences of the foundational disintegration we have been experiencing since the War for Southern Independence.

Now more than ever, and in the face of insidious political correctness, ideological delusion, a widespread Pollyanna mentality, and pervasive historical revisionism, our foundational governing principles and rights demand our clear-headed attention and vigorous assertion if we are to successfully survive the political treachery which has befallen us. If we genuinely cherish those principles and rights, then it remains our duty to defend and advance them in any way we can. If history is any lesson, once lost, only the clash of arms can again restore those principles and rights. And in that regard, we can only hope that such a painful re-learning of history's lessons can be averted.

If we can prevent national dissolution by restoring constitutional order throughout the land, all well and good. But, ALL appropriate Founder-sanctioned remedies to successfully counter the malignant deconstruction of our system of governance must be on the table. That said, my personal view is that, short of a miracle, the foundational deterioration of our republican-free enterprise system is so nearly complete as to render that corruption irreversible, the consequence of which is that the successful restoration of constitutional order on a national level is most likely unattainable. Not a Pollyanna by nature, I am, therefore, expecting the deterioration to worsen, but am both hoping and working to reverse this corrosive process. So, while I'm not throwing in the towel just yet, I am refocusing on more realistic and achievable outcomes. And that is precisely what we should all be doing. But, for starters, we must all jettison the blinders which dangerously impair our ability to clearly see conditions as they really are.

So, to clear-eyed patriots everywhere: don't be overwhelmed into compliance by the lawlessness, double-talk, chicanery and propaganda spewed by our "leaders" and their minions; keep your eyes on the ball and be prepared for further painful and dramatic change. Very importantly, however, begin developing a workable plan to survive and prevail as Freemen. My suggestion is that we take careful measure of those States within the current union which are most likely to successfully succeed as independent republican states. It's always a good idea to know where best to relocate our families when the rubber really does hit the road.

Our choice is simple: weak-kneed, mindless submission to and continued accommodation with an alien order quite at odds with our founding principles *or* a single-minded commitment to restoring constitutional order--if not on a broad national level, then on a State or regional/ confederated level. In any event, I can only hope that most Americans will clearly see the subversion taking place, make no excuses for it, and finally take appropriate action to reverse course.

Watching our republic slip into oblivion, I wonder just what it will take to rouse Americans from their stupor? What will it take to encourage them to take convincing remedial action to shake up the power structure and to actually resurrect the republic. I'm still wondering, and I'm still without an answer. I don't pretend to have the solution, but I do know that our doing more of the same, i.e. a little more than nothing, solves just that: nothing!

(*"Any people, anywhere, being inclined and having the power, have the right to rise up and shake off the existing government, and form a new one that suits them better. This is a most valuable, a most sacred right, a right which we hope and believe is to liberate the world."* A. Lincoln on the floor of the US House of Representatives, 1847.)

(*"The powers not delegated to the United States by the Constitution, nor prohibited by it to the States, are reserved to the States respectively, or to the people."* Amendment X of the US Constitution, 1791)

(*"If any state in the Union will declare that it prefers separation...to a continuance in the union...I have no hesitation in saying, 'let us separate.'"* Thomas Jefferson)

("...a breach of any one article [of the Constitution] by any one party, leaves all other parties at liberty to consider the whole convention as dissolved." James Madison, The Madison Papers)

(Evaluating Lincoln's inspiring Gettysburg words that Union soldiers sacrificed their lives to the cause of self-determination, i.e. government of, by and for the people, H. L. Mencken asserted that *the Union soldiers in the battle actually fought against self-determination; it was the Confederates who fought for the right of people to govern themselves.")*

("If tyranny and despotism justified the Revolution of 1776, then we do not see why it would not justify the secession of Five Millions of Southrons from the Federal Union in 1861." New York Tribune, 1860)

Just Say "NO MORE!!!"

After a few years trying to write what I had hoped were some sober and reasonably dispassionate posts, to start things off allow me the luxury of simply blowing off steam for a moment. Hey, it's therapeutic.

Anyone willing to take the time to honestly and objectively examine Obama's mysterious background and his obvious un-American associations, statements and actions over the years should be justifiably troubled and incensed. Only if one is completely brain-dead or otherwise hopelessly disengaged can one fail to share this anger and trepidation.

Only willfully ignorant, soulless political hacks and self-serving recipients of public largess and political favors are still capable of shamelessly and delusionally denying the obvious: Marxism has taken hold in the highest rungs of our government; the feds are out-of-control and unrepresentative; Congress has abdicated far too many of its constitutional responsibilities to an increasingly imperial Presidency and to his unaccountable and unelected bureaucrats; we the people, the States and our "representatives" have allowed an activist and unaccountable judiciary to repeatedly flout the Constitution with impunity and to arbitrarily dictate the original meaning and intent of the Constitution. As a result, our rights and liberties have been diminished and our economy drained of its vitality and promise.

There are times when citizens need to fearlessly speak up, stand tall, be boldly honest about what's clearly going on around them, and be willing to be criticized for their principles and integrity. And, yes, if need be they must even be willing to sacrifice their own lives in defense of America and the Republic for which it stands.

As Lincoln asserted, "Silence makes cowards out of the best of men." Thus, if we are to resurrect our Republic, we must reject our hitherto squeamish silence in the face of growing tyranny.

For those who care to do any honest and objective research, historical evidence irrefutably demonstrates that for decades the Progressive/Socialist/Marxist movement in America has ruthlessly sought the undermining of American culture by systematically eroding patriotism, morality, the sanctity of the family and spiritual beliefs, the cultural building blocks of the most exceptional, wealthiest and freest nation the world has ever known—well, at least up until recently, that is.

Toward achievement of his utopian ends, Obama, true to his pre-inaugural pledge to his vacuous fawning fans who ignorantly propelled him into office, has stuck like glue to his plan of "fundamentally transforming the United States of America". And, tragically, he and his Progressive disciples are but a hair's breath away from fully accomplishing this iniquitous goal.

With the connivance of, among others, ACORN, ACLU, NEA, Nat'l Socialists of America, the **Progressive Congressional Caucus**, the Environmentalist Movement, a complicit leftist-dominated media which has morphed into a propaganda mouthpiece for the Progressive agenda, bubble-headed Hollywood elites, all manner of Soros-funded socialist front organizations, and a veritable throng of what Lenin succinctly dubbed "useful idiots" on the left, Obama, whose eligibility still remains in serious doubt, was re-elected in 2012 rendering his subversive anti-American Marxist makeover intact and on course.

We must bear in mind that neither Obama nor his Progressive minions, aka Marxists, will stop at <u>anything</u> to ensure that America as we know it has been completely transformed into a socialist utopia with these thugs at its helm. And even had Obama not been re-elected, it will still require years of conscientious effort to undo the nearly incalculable damage already wrought by these ideological vermin.

Any sober student of history knows full well and without equivocation that Socialism and Communism have been and will always be notorious failures and painfully costly in both blood and treasure. We know that Socialism is meant for the masses, not for the elites who impose it on the rest of us. At the people's expense, the governing elites will manage to live in the lap of luxury while we lowly plebeians are compelled to eke out a living in the Progressive's fetid egalitarian paradise.

Like oil and water, **Marxism and liberty simply cannot peacefully co-exist**. The Progressive ideology is the implacable enemy of this country's traditions, values and republican form of governance. And for patriots to attempt to accommodate or otherwise appease this alien ideology is not only suicidal, but as treasonous as Progressivism itself. (Let's no longer shirk from calling Progressivism, aka Modern Liberalism, what it really is: the enemy within.)

It's well past time to say NO MORE!!! It is well past time to fully take back our country or risk irretrievably losing it in its entirety for ourselves and our posterity.

If the ballot box no longer serves the purpose of effectively safeguarding liberty and restoring constitutional order, then patriots must be fully prepared to courageously, proudly and unyieldingly resort to Civil Disobedience.

States must unhesitatingly and boldly assert their 10th Amendment authority to nullify unconstitutional laws/edicts/rulings regardless of the offending federal branch which originates them.

And if these forms of constitutional resistance somehow fail to restore constitutional order then secession must be on the table if we are to prevent Progressives from denying all Americans their rights to life, liberty and the pursuit of happiness.

I urge all patriots to unashamedly and fearlessly assert their God-given unalienable rights by putting this government on notice that we're not going to take it anymore.

At every turn, liberal insanity and noxious political correctness must be confronted head-on. No more backing off merely to achieve a hollow sense of "getting along". No more indoctrination of our youth and no more government profligacy to advance parochial political and alien ideological agendas.

If this means massive marches on Washington and even occupation of our government buildings, insisting that our state legislatures summarily nullify ALL unconstitutional laws/edicts/rulings emanating from our runaway and Marxist-infected federal government, openly disobeying/ignoring federal rules, assertively restoring illegally held federal lands to the States, and drilling without federal sanction, among other appropriate acts of lawful and rightful defiance, then so be it. The restoration of constitutional order and economic sanity must be our rigidly unshakeable goals.

I've said it before, and I'm saying it again: **an indivisible union at any price may prove to be too high a price to pay for a free people,** and submitting to federal overreach merely to "keep the peace" or "to get along" is empty-headed and, ultimately, self-destructive. If we can't enjoy constitutional order in all the states, then let's enjoy it in at least a portion of those states. And if that means secession, a time-honored constitutional and God-given right enshrined in our Declaration of Independence, then let's seriously begin that conversation now before we are all lulled into a quagmire of submission and oppression from which there will be little chance for peaceful deliverance.

We must also remain actively engaged in grassroots patriotic organizations and **do what we can to link ourselves and our organizations with other patriotic groups around the country,** this to enhance our credibility and to more effectively influence our nation's course. And, naturally, we should continue to be actively involved in local politics to help restore our party's respect for and adherence to constitutional principles.

Guided by the Constitution and biblical precepts, we must fearlessly speak up with clarity, knowledge, and commonsense. Fearlessly speaking truth to power should become second nature. And remember this: the Constitution cannot defend itself. That responsibility ultimately rests with We the People.

Silence in the face of tyranny is cowardice and, worse, treasonous. Facing down liberal elites is the height of honor and patriotism. Do it!

("The tree of liberty must be refreshed from time to time with the blood of patriots and tyrants; the strongest reason for the people to retain the right to keep and bear arms is, as a last resort, to protect themselves against tyranny in government." Thomas Jefferson)

How to Stop Progressive Tyranny COLD (1/2013)

For some time now, I have speculated as to what can be done to effectively counter the unrelenting Progressive onslaught on our liberties and individual sovereignty.

Sincerely believing that, at long last, Progressives must be boldly and constitutionally challenged and outmaneuvered, and thinking outside the proverbial box, I think I've come up with a plan worth pursuing. But, like any political action plan worth its salt, so much depends upon the commitment, political courage and integrity of some key political players. (Sadly, that requirement could be this plan's Achilles' heel.)

To counter Progressive tyranny, many States are finally getting a spine and asserting their sovereignty by actually nullifying federal laws and bureucratic rulings. And someday soon I hope judicial activist rulings are similarly resisted as well. And if rule of law is our goal, then **State Nullification** remains an indispensable tool in our quiver of remedies.

From a historical standpoint, the sheer volume of nullification activities over the last four years exceeds anything this country has seen since before the War of Northern Aggression, aka the War of Southern Secession in 1861, misleadingly dubbed the "civil war". A very hopeful trend, indeed, and a trend we should all endorse and encourage. For as Thomas Jefferson asserted, nullification is "the rightful remedy" to federal encroachment. (Note: with the fearless and dedicated efforts of the 10th Amendment Center, I suspect that acts of nullification, interposition and anti-commandeering will be on the upswing in the years ahead. And thank God for that!)

Of course, there's **impeachment** to stop the madness. However, impeachment's a fine idea ONLY if we can be assured of conviction and removal as well. Otherwise, an impeachment process will, for the most part, be of little consequence. And with the Senate firmly in the hands of the Progressives and squeamish RINOs (Republicans-in-Name-Only), I suspect only outright acts of treason or murder by a Chief Executive would convince enough Senators to actually convict and remove. (In truth, however, since Progressives are inherently ruthless and unprincipled, I'm not sure even murder or treason would do the trick these days.) Thus, I think we can safely conclude that impeachment alone cannot be relied upon to effectively remedy federal lawlessness. But that's not saying it shouldn't be seriously attempted.

So, here's what I propose. It's a simple, doable and powerful antidote to subversive federal excesses. More importantly, this plan, if faithfully implemented, will eliminate the need for outright rebellion or secession, unsettling prospects which, in the absence of effective grassroots resistance and political courage at the top, have become increasingly credible.

1. **Call for Nullification**: Bearing in mind that We the People and our immediate fiduciary agents, the States, creators of this union, are the ultimate arbiters of what is and what is not constitutional, when the White House or any department of the Executive Branch issues an unconstitutional order or directive, or if the Supreme Court issues a ruling which is clearly unconstitutional, and the offending entity refuses to rescind that order, directive or ruling, the <u>Speaker of the House and the Senate Minority Leader</u> must urgently and publicly appeal to the several States to nullify those encroachments straightaway. In effect, these key leaders must boldly circumvent federal perpetrators of lawlessness by <u>using their bully pulpits</u> to exhort the States and the People to disobey and to appropriately resist.

If the States refuse to comply with or cooperate in the enforcement (anti-commandeering) of those unlawful orders/rulings/directives, for all practical purposes the federal actions are of no force and the feds will have no choice but to back off in those jurisdictions where nullification or anti-commandeering has been invoked. Such resistance will, as envisioned by the Founders, help restore the balance of power between the States and the federal government. Further, this would place us back on the road to constitutional order and dramatically restore public trust in our representatives.

In their **bully pulpit appeals**, congressional leaders must clearly explain why such resistance is necessary and constitutionally justified, explicating in vivid and understandable detail the natural/unalienable rights of man, the principles of State sovereignty and the balance of powers doctrine, all of which are enshrined in our Constitution. And, of course, their exhortations must include a concise explanation of the 10th Amendment.

And if these national leaders choose not to take such dramatic action, which I suspect might well be the case, then State Senators/Representatives should promptly and boldly assume this patriotic responsibility for their respective States. In short, the President is not the only political leader with a bully pulpit. All political leaders have bully pulpits, and they must all use them to help restore constitutional order.

2. **Appeal to Sheriffs**: In their appeals to the country, and as appropriate to the nature of the federal excess, political leaders at the both the federal state levels should directly exhort all Sheriffs to uphold their oath of office by refusing to comply with or enforce any and all unconstitutional orders/directives within their jurisdiction from whatever source, state or federal.

3. **Impeachment & Withholding of Funds:** In parallel, the federal and state legislatures should deny funding to the offending office and immediately invoke articles of impeachment against the offending federal or state officials--not merely threaten to impeach, but formally act to both impeach and remove. This should also include heretofore untouchable, unaccountable sitting justices and judges.

4. Concurrently, **take the perpetrators of federal excess to court.**

This entirely lawful and principled 4-pronged approach to remedying Progressive overreach and restoring constitutional order would stop the heretofore unchecked Progressive contagion cold, and the authority of the People will be restored.

In the meantime, patriotic organizations around the country should continue to unite, monitor both federal and State excesses, and appropriately initiate, support and coordinate national resistance wherever federal or State excesses occur.

For whatever good it does, I shared this proposal with the offices of both the Speaker and the Senate Majority Leader. I also copied in Sen. Lee of Utah and Sen. Rand Paul of Kentucky. How much political courage and boldness in defense of liberty they may be willing to muster remains to be seen.

Only political courage and lawful, bold, intensive and assertive patriotic activism at all levels can avert political and economic disaster. The alternative for us, of course, is more appeasement, accommodation and, eventually, servitude. Which course will we choose?

At long last, ACTION and PATRIOTISM must be more than words. "Let's roll!"

Is It Too Late to Restore Constitutional Order? (7/2012)

Though the first sentence in Article II of the Constitution provides that "executive Power shall be vested in a President of the United States of America", none of the Framers or Ratifiers suggested at any time that this sentence would entail any executive authority beyond those specific powers enumerated in Sections 2 and 3.

In short, presidential powers are well-defined and limited to faithfully executing the laws passed by Congress and, with proper legislative oversight, to preside over foreign affairs. A Chief Executive's violating these obligations was determined by the Founders to be a "breach of trust" and, therefore, grounds for impeachment and removal from office.

Clearly, over the years, executive powers under both Democrat and Republican chief executives have grown exponentially to the extent that the range of those powers exercised would stagger our republican Founders. (That said, the extent to which Barack Obama has usurped authority is beyond just staggering. His actions in this regard have been manifestly impeachable. And it is my guess that should bonafide conservatives sweep both the House and Senate, this and other Presidents of his ilk in the future stand a better than even chance of facing impeachment and removal from office. And despite the civil and political unrest that might ensue from such a justifiable remedial action, impeachment is precisely what our Founders and the Constitution they crafted would have counseled.)

So, how did this dangerous expansion of presidential powers come to pass? Very simply, because government, a creature of human nature, is, if ineffectively checked, predisposed to expanding its authority and power. And in designing the Constitution, the Framers were painfully aware of and warned against this natural tendency toward centralization and, ultimately, tyranny. Not surprisingly, despite their warnings we've permitted ourselves to slip into the clutches of authoritarianism and lawlessness.

For whatever reason--much of it having to do with the enormous growth in the federal government and its expansion into areas never envisioned by the Founders or sanctioned by the Constitution--Congress has ceded or otherwise delegated enormous powers to the Executive Branch and, by extension, to that branch's officers and departments. The catastrophic result of this irresponsible congressional delegation of powers is twofold: an imperial presidency and an essentially unchecked and nearly omnipotent federal bureaucracy which, in a real sense, has been permitted to operate outside constitutional constraints.

Thus, we must now accept the reality that "throwing the bums out" in Congress is no longer a viable remedy; it is merely a desperate, shortsighted and delusional reformist's rallying cry "full of sound and fury, signifying nothing". In truth, only if the wings of the Executive Branch are clipped and the unbridled federal bureaucracy is both drastically downsized and more properly supervised by Congress, "the people's house", can genuine constitutional order be restored.

Tragically, what NO ONE has been seriously talking about is the need to rein in BOTH the Executive Branch and Leviathan's runaway bureaucracy which, in combination, have been eating away at the very vitals of our republic. Only by assertively restricting presidential powers to those which faithfully comport with the Constitution, and only by both eliminating or drastically reducing the power of the federal bureaucracy can our inexorable slide toward tyranny be averted.

Is it too late? Probably. And if that's the case, then the several States, at the insistence of an aroused citizenry, should re-examine their unhealthy association with an increasingly corrosive central government no longer faithful to the Constitution or to the People. In faithful pursuit of constitutional order, States must understand that they are duty-bound to protect their citizens from federal overreach and, if necessary, to strike out on their own, eventually allying themselves with like-minded sister States.

Thus, the burning question for me is this: no matter the terrible price one must pay, should a patriot who values his liberty continue to routinely and blindly submit to the self-destructive, albeit high-sounding, Lincolnesque notion of "indivisible unity"? Not no. But, Hell no!

Unless constitutional order at the national level is restored, I dare say that disunion ought, of necessity, be embraced. And given the chasmic ideological divide currently existing in the country, I really don't believe disunion is anything but inevitable.

("I am not a friend to a very energetic government. It is always oppressive; most bad government has grown out of too much government; the natural progress of things is for liberty to yield and government to gain ground." Thomas Jefferson)

("When in the course of human events, it becomes necessary for one people to dissolve the political bands which have connected them with another, and to assume among the powers of the earth, the separate and equal station to which the Laws of Nature and of Nature's God entitle them, a decent respect to the opinions of mankind requires that they should declare the cause which impel them to the separation." (<u>Declaration of Independence</u>, July 4, 1776)

What If...? (10/2012)

On patriotic internet sites, I often read about the heart-felt frustration in readers' comments over both the unchecked lawlessness of the federal government as well as the painful absence of effective and concerted remedial action on the part of patriots everywhere to correct those abuses.

WHAT IF Obama stubbornly continues on his reckless course to "fundamentally transform the US of A"?

WHAT IF he, his progressive allies and the acquiescent politicians on the other side of the political aisle continue to ignore and, by their neglect, enable the federal government's continuing to routinely flout and undermine the US Constitution with impunity?

My sense is that for millions of patriots, the prospect of many more years of progressive tyranny would be a bridge too far. Backs to the wall and fearing for their lives, liberties and their ability to pursue happiness, my guess is that these patriots would, with proper leadership and in a spirit of civic-mindedness, tenaciously and unselfishly commit to taking all appropriate action to arrest America's march toward progressive tyranny.

With the Constitution as their guide, among these countless patriots, political accommodation, appeasement and compromise would be adjudged odious, self-destructive and, yes, treasonous. Seriously committed to restoring constitutional and economic order as well as to safeguarding and re-applying the foundational doctrines of "separation of powers" and "checks and balances", my guess is that the resulting societal and political impact on the nation would be historical in both scope and intensity.

At least, that is my fervent hope.

Short of rebellion, the question becomes how can patriots effectively push back and stop the Progressive steamroller, failing which Americans everywhere must, by their ineffective action or silence, reconcile themselves to subservience to the federal leviathan?

While I'm sure my proposal doesn't break new ground, here it is anyway:

First and foremost, to be effective, organized patriotic resistance must be rigidly guided by participants' unwavering and fearless pledge to uphold, defend and fully implement the original meaning and intent of the Constitution of the United States as well as the Constitutions of the several States. Importantly, personal agendas cannot be permitted to play any part whatsoever.

Second, to effectively counter the power elite, and while retaining their independence from one another, patriotic organizations around the country must link up and pledge their "patriotic cooperation" with the aim of effecting a reversal of progressive tyranny and restoration of constitutional governance from the ground up.

Third, all patriotic organizations should, at some point soon, immediately dispatch representatives to a "national convention of patriots" (ironic were it to be convened in Philadelphia) to develop both a list of grievances, again firmly grounded in the Constitution and our founding documents—and not driven by short-sighted parochialism or self-aggrandizement--and a corresponding list of specific strategies for well-coordinated nationwide activist engagement and, as necessary, civil disobedience and other forms of appropriate and meaningful resistance.

Among countless strategies, this initial grassroots agenda might well entail widespread refusal to pay various taxes/fees whose payment would constitute a clear violation of the Constitution; actively resisting EPA bullying by on-site demonstrations of solidarity with those job-creating industries (coal, gas) which have been especially injured by EPA overreach; resisting BLM; developing a draft of Article V Convention of States reforms; pressing State legislative representatives to resist federal overreach and to encourage States to immediately assume control over and to drill for oil/gas in those federal lands illegally held by the federal government. Obviously, the possibilities are endless. But, you get the drift.

Representatives might opt to extend invitations to reputable constitutional scholars and historians to elicit their input, counsel and participation as well.

The burning question is what reputable organizers of which creditable patriotic organizations already in existence who already enjoy notoriety and a following are willing to take the lead in this patriotic networking effort? What knowledgeable organizers are willing to initiate contacts with other national and local grassroots patriotic organizations to propose this patriotic networking and convention of patriots? Who's willing to step up? All we need is leadership to pull it together.

Finally, this: why wouldn't a "National Patriot Convention"--not a constitutional convention--be entirely appropriate? Both progressivism, the enemy of republicanism, and an unscrupulous disregard for and ignorance of the original meaning of the Constitution on the part of our other political elites—both on the left and right—constitute an insidious contagion, a "clear and present danger" which imperils both our way of life and our republican form of government.

If, indeed, and as provided for in the Constitution and by the framers and ratifiers of same, We the People are the final arbiters of what is and what is not constitutional, and if We the People are, in fact, sovereign and preeminent in this republican system of government, then the duty rests squarely on our shoulders to remedy the "train of abuses".

No more excuses. No more inaction. No more let-the-other-guy-do-it. No more therapeutically preaching or venting to the choir. Going forward, we must fully understand that only active, constructive, effective and **unified** nationwide grassroots engagement will turn the authoritarian tide and restore constitutional order.

I pray someone of national prominence and credibility steps up to help move this grassroots effort forward. Allen West? Tom Coburn? Tea Party organizers/blog managers? Who knows? So many excellent possibilities too numerous to suggest here.

Truth is millions of patriots are chomping at the bit to make a REAL difference. Individually, we are reduced to whining, frustrated victims of tyranny. United, well-coordinated and firm in our civic-minded conviction to restore public trust and constitutional order, we millions are a powerhouse and can substantively influence the direction both of our States and of our nation.

If the threat of Progressive political dominion in the future doesn't spur us to effectively act in patriotic concert, just what will—ever? Doing nothing is a surefire recipe for disaster, a tacit consent to tyranny.

("What country can preserve its liberties if its rulers are not warned from time to time that their people preserve the spirit of resistance?" Thomas Jefferson)

("The two enemies of the people are criminals and government, so let us tie the second down with the chains of the Constitution so the second will not become the legalized version of the first." Thomas Jefferson)

("Whenever the legislators endeavor to take away and destroy the property of the people, or to reduce them to slavery under arbitrary power, they put themselves into a state of war with the people, who are thereupon absolved from any further obedience." John Locke)

[2] KNOW YOUR ENEMY

Understanding Modern Liberals: Know the Enemy

I knew that flinging my shoes and casting profanities at the parade of sneering and unctuous liberal talking heads and spinmeisters on TV simply had to stop. I realized I had to take control of my reactions or run the risk of either ruining a perfectly good TV set or subjecting myself to a costly regimen of antidepressants.

Long annoyed and distressed by liberal hypocrisy, mendacity, arrogance, recklessly muddled thinking, and, for me, their barely concealed contempt for the proverbial unwashed masses for whom they insincerely profess empathy and solidarity, I decided to at least somewhat mitigate my irritation by better understanding what liberals were REALLY all about. By better understanding why they behave as they do, I figured I'd be better able to more objectively deal with them and to control my reactions to them. Regaining my composure and keeping my blood pressure in check were my goals.

By attempting to psychologically define the stereotypical modern liberal I felt I would no longer be unduly stressed by their grossly sophomoric view of reality, intolerable smugness, reckless irresponsibility, their authoritarian proclivities, childish rants and scurrilous ad hominem. Thus, my quest for answers.

Much to my surprise and relief, a respectable amount of thoughtful research on this very question has been compiled by many fine writers, historians and psychologists, many names of whom I have simply forgotten. But, among them are luminaries like Eric Hoffer, whom I had always considered the working man's philosopher and whose brilliant and penetrating books about mass movements and ideologies I so thoroughly enjoyed both in my high school and college years.

To gain a better understanding, I also relied on the insights of Dr. Lyle Rossiter, author of "The Liberal Mind", Eric Alan Beltt, writer for Frontiers of Freedom, John Ray, contributor to Front Page Magazine (and my most illuminating resource), as well as a number of other thoughtful writers, professionals and thinkers.

First, a brief definition of liberalism:

"Classical Liberalism" generally refers to the liberalism existing before the 20th century which emphasizes rational self-interest, limited republican government, individual moral and social responsibility, equal opportunity, free markets and the inherent rights of individuals to pursue life, liberty and property. (Think America's founders.)

Classical Liberalism shouldn't be confused with "modern liberalism" which de-emphasizes the individual by advocating the predominant role of the state via collective class and group action.

Classical Liberals espouse the concept of "negative rights" meaning an individual's freedom from the coercive actions of government and other people. Conversely, modern liberals adhere to the concept of "positive rights", meaning that government should determine the rights of individuals. Classical liberalism more closely resembles conservatism and libertarianism while modern liberalism embodies socialist and collectivist principles. Modern liberals are more inclined to violate the rules of natural law and of human nature by attempting to impose behavioral/attitudinal norms and intellectual standards by way of paternalistic state-directed collectivism.

That said, Alan Beltt posits in one of his essays that "liberalism isn't a political ideology; it's a psychology – the psychology of self-satisfaction to be precise." This fundamental assertion is worth remembering as we move forward.

According to Beltt, a liberal ideologue's thinking is driven by an aversion to being excluded and by a powerful desire "to feel intelligent, moral, noble, or unique, as well as a desire for peer acceptance and reverence", but Belt cautions that this characterization of a liberal ideologue is quite apart from the non-activist self-identified liberal who may, from time to time, give the appearance of agreement with liberal ideologues owing to parochial self-interest or simply ignorance, e.g. an otherwise politically conservative member of a teacher's union.

Belt states that the liberal ideologues' common bond is "their straight-forward simplicity" which shuns "real solutions to real problems." (Like the government takeover of healthcare in order to expand healthcare services and reduce costs without affecting the quality of healthcare.)

Further, he reasons that the causes for which a liberal fights is "relevant only insofar as different causes stroke different needs [like] moral superiority, intellectual superiority, group acceptance, aversion to emotional trauma, etc." Wow! Sounds eerily akin to an adolescent's emotional and psychological profile, huh?

Beltt goes on to assert that because liberals are so concerned about their egos that they tend to gravitate to academia, news and entertainment, and the legal professions; that since "liberals want to be society's elite and powerful" being a part of an elite circle is extremely important to them; that *because they want to feel good about themselves they're wholly dependent upon how others feel about them.* Thus, what better way to earn others' respect and acceptance than by being a successful academician, entertainer or lawyer, etc. So, I guess it can be safely said that emotional immaturity and a child-like need for peer acceptance are dominant liberal indicators.

To feel a sense of superiority, liberals unquestionably regard the poor, the uneducated, southerners, conservatives, religious people, and minorities as inferior. (Remember Obama's arrogant "clinging to their guns and religion" screed?) By feeding the poor and downtrodden, liberals seek expressions of gratitude and praise, and, in turn, an affirmation of their superiority, which is, of course, their overarching goal. Wow! It's finally coming together. Adolescents in adult bodies yearning for acceptance and recognition.

Liberals continually regard international acceptance and popularity as a must. (Obama's "apology tour" come to mind.) Why? Because one can't feel morally and intellectually superior if others don't look up to you. To the liberal, then, personal affirmation, avoiding personal consequences and unpopularity invariably take precedence over national security. This fits nicely with the modern liberal's opposition to "unilateral action" since negative consequences of unilateral actions would fall squarely upon them rendering them morally accountable to their international elitist peers. Oh, the shame.

Conversely, any negative consequences of "multilateralism" can be shared with their liberal allies around the world. (Thus, their unstinting support of the UN and other international/globalist organizations.) So, in short, it's really all about ego. Thus, it seems that some of us simply never outgrow our adolescent insecurities.

Beltt nicely illustrates the egotism of liberals by describing the manner in which they argue and debate. As he succinctly observes, "to conservatives, debate is about issues…but to liberals it is about them." Ah! Now I get it. Like debating with a self-centered, insecure teenager.

In a debate, the liberal "either wants to prove his superiority or the other person's inferiority, or both", and rather than lose the debate, the liberal invariably relies on ad hominem, wild-eyed claims of bigotry, and evasion—the psychological defense mechanisms of the insecure and the narcissist.

Obviously, this can be very infuriating to the unwary classical liberal, conservative or libertarian who seeks substantive dialogue and fact-based solutions. For liberals, however, the purpose of politics is to stoke their egos, and political power is the ultimate affirmation of that superiority. So, in a very real sense, political power is the means to personal gratification. Thus, it's likely disturbingly true that genuinely selfless service is very much an alien motivator for most liberals, but, I'm sure, for some other politicians of different political stripes as well. Gee! I'm feeling better already. Knowledge really is power. So, in effect, what I (and you) have been dealing with are neurotic me-first kids in adult bodies. Nothing more and nothing less.

Finally, Beltt suggests that liberals tend to be "intellectually lazy". Their fixation with "shades of gray" and moral relativism is stereotypically liberal which inevitably leads to ethereal and feel-good answers that merely "sound right" (like affirmative action, gun control, socialized healthcare, anti-war movements, aversion to tax cuts) but which are, if more carefully weighed, simply illogical or intellectually indefensible.

Relying upon rational thought clearly means abandoning their pursuit of affirmation, a frightening risk the liberal would surely avoid like the plague. And since deeply delving into an opponent's argument could factually disprove a liberal's position and thus diminish his sense of intellectual superiority, such an intellectual exercise would, of course, be routinely avoided. And since "it is much easier [for a liberal] to just assume someone has different values than it is to try to understand why they believe what they believe," I have to wonder if a typical liberal would as objectively examine the conservative mind as non-liberals have examined the liberal mind. Very doubtful, as this would require some uncomfortable level of self-examination and self-discovery as well. Oops. Can't have that.

Moving on, John Ray posits that "Rightists [as opposed to Leftists] have no need either for change or its opposite and may oppose change if they see it as destructive or favor change if they see it as constructive." To liberals, however, their motive for changing society is to "draw attention to themselves…as being wise, innovative, caring, etc."

In a somewhat less tempered manner, Mr. Ray discusses a variety of liberal positions which, for him, illustrate the liberal phenomenon:

1. *Human Nature*: Leftists reject the immutability of human nature and heredity. To the liberal, virtually all human behavior can be molded and shaped, and acquired characteristics can be genetically passed on. (Among other things, this might well explain their attachment to high-minded "restorative justice", social engineering and their single-minded attempt to dominate public education.)

2. *The Church*: Leftists are generally antagonistic toward ecclesiastical authorities which "enforce conventional morality" for the purpose of ensuring societal and familial order. Having infiltrated many churches, secular Leftists hope to further erode Christian power and influence while expanding their own. (For example, the accommodation of same-sex marriage on the part of some churches today is illustrative of this infiltration.) Leftists generally favor abortion, contraception, those

more primitive religions which are less threatening, and oppose religious schooling and financial support for parochial schools. To Ray, Liberals attempt "to exploit Judeo-Christian teachings of love and compassion [in order to] promote the usual Leftist goals of enforced equality."

3. *Anti-Racist Hypocrisy*: liberals camouflage their own anti-Semitism and racism by viciously and unrelentingly attacking others who disagree with them for harboring those feelings. (Classic Psych 101 "transference".) Marx, Hitler and Stalin, among other Leftists, were notoriously anti-Semitic and racist and always justified their actions in the name of "the people". It's worth noting that all the mass murders of the 20th century were perpetrated by Leftists and "virulent racism" can and does, in fact, exist on the Left. Spiro Agnew described Leftists as "limousine liberals" who seldom opt to actually live in neighborhoods with a sizable number of minority residents. Also to Ray, the profusion of documentaries about Hitler in the liberal dominated media and the relative paucity of documentaries about Stalin attest to the Left's barely disguised "obsession" with Nazism. This is not to say that modern liberals are Nazis, only that they are cut from the same psychological cloth.

4. *Racism*: liberals "tend to characterize as racist almost anyone who is honest about his or her perfectly normal feelings of group identity." Why? To earn personal acclaim for their compassion and adherence to "equality" and, of course, to weaken inter-group cohesiveness. (Race-baiting is a means to divide and conquer.)

With respect to Americans and capitalism, Ray sees an uncomfortable commonality of disenchantment among liberals, Muslim fanatics, and "Green" extremists. He also examines the Left's hypocritical level of intensity when it comes to strongly condemning European or Western "atrocities" (like the "infamous" Abu Graib, Guantanamo, America's treatment of illegal aliens) while seldom excoriating Pol Pot's "killing fields", Stalin's "gulag", Japan's raping and pillaging of China, Kim Il Sung's death camps, and a whole host of "mini-holocausts" perpetrated in Africa and other areas of the world.)

5. *Equality & Moral Equivalence*: "In the name of bringing about equality, Leftists get an excuse to tear down the whole of existing structure of society—something that they need to do to give themselves any chance

of fulfilling their dream of taking over all power for themselves. It is the fact that they are not in charge of everything that the leftist most of all wants to change." The so-called "dumbing down" of America's educational system and the accent on promoting self-esteem over healthy competition and achievement is an excellent example of liberalism's enforced equality. Exempted, of course, are the liberal elites themselves who foist defective public education standards on the general public while dispatching their children to private schools. You'll notice that school vouchers are robustly opposed by the left.

This pursuit of "equality" invariably leads to their advocacy of redistribution of income, progressive taxation, inheritance and death taxes, generous foreign aid, feminism, cap and trade, gay rights, and socialized medicine. Further, Leftists express their amoral belief in "moral equivalence" by, for example, asserting the moral equivalence--or equivalent blameworthiness or praiseworthiness--of Islamic terrorists and Christian fundamentalists. Mr. Ray describes their amorality as "the mark of a psychopath--the moral imbecile" which simply can't tell the difference between right and wrong and, therefore, cannot be held accountable for any brutality and unpleasantness which might result from such simplistic and coldhearted shallowness. This sounds eerily akin to the way our justice system views underage criminals, huh? So, it shouldn't surprise us that KSM and his terrorist buddies are being accorded due-process protections and trial by a civilian court in NYC.

6. *Political Correctness*: leftists attempt to change our views of other groups by arbitrarily altering the words we use to describe them, e.g. undocumented immigrant vs. illegal alien, but also by ensuring the inability of airport security to more carefully examine those who are more likely than other racial groups to pose a terrorist threat, and by willfully ignoring the militant Islamism and anti-Americanism of the infamous Maj. Hassan all in the name of empty-headed "diversity", etc. So, while they talk a good game about breaking down barriers, providing a "big tent" and encouraging an open discussion of racial and cultural differences, the Leftist's real game is to quash honest dialogue, knowledge and debate in order to divide and dominate.

7. *The Leftist Appeal*: "liberals are attracted to absurd offers of something for nothing; their sense of equality is motivated more by their goal

of bringing those in power down than to raising everyone up. As for the elitist power structure itself, its real goal is to be more equal than others." A good example of this is the Communist Party in the USSR to whose members special privileges, goods and services were accorded to the exclusion of other Soviet citizens.

8. *Guilt v Compassion*: expressions or demonstrations of liberal compassion are dictated by "a desire for self-righteousness, praise, power and excitement" and not by any genuine sense of guilt. Selfishly motivated, the typical liberal expects government—not themselves--to finance liberal expressions of compassion. Thus, their overarching goal is power and influence, not the betterment of mankind.

9. *Religion*: now more than ever, Mr. Ray clearly believes that Leftism has in many ways evolved into a secular religion. In universities, "Marxism is often treated as a theology" whose every wisdom is so carefully examined by professorial keepers of the faith. Through this brainwashing, the goal of liberals is to eclipse the power and influence of the church. Generally, liberals want churches to serve their agenda so that liberalism's political domination can be more readily achieved. Like in spiritual based religions, Leftists too need to believe in things which sound good even if they cannot be proven.

10. *Other Causes of Liberalism*: especially to impressionable youth seeking peer acceptance, "heroic" advocacy of human rights and the needs of the downtrodden is "cool"; the fraudulent appeal of easy or simple solutions to complex problems and the need for instant self-gratification; the need for acceptance by non-conformists, misfits, pacifists, social pariahs, idealists, malcontents, fanatics, the ambitious, the bored and "the weird". (Eric Hoffer figured this out long ago.)

11. *Leftists in Academe*: since the humanities and social science schools of US colleges and universities are "monopolized" by liberals, these schools "are intolerant of diversity, opposed to free speech, and discriminatory in their hiring practices." (In others words, conservatives need not apply.) However, Mr. Ray reassuringly notes that given that most intelligent graduates go into the business world (real world) rather than the teaching field (theoretical world), and that there are now many alternative sources of information (broadcasting)

currently dominating the American scene, liberalism's impact on most graduates is, fortunately, fleeting. (But, keep your eye on the FCC which, in the hands of Progressives, will always attempt to curtail or altogether eliminate divergent viewpoints on the airwaves.)

12. *Egotism*: thinking well of oneself is, in general, healthy; however, excessive self-satisfaction or self-esteem is abnormal and can lead to criminal behavior, a misplaced entitlement mentality, an irrational sense of superiority, elitism, a cavalier attitude toward others, a simplistic and unrealistic understanding of the forces at play in our lives, a neurotic need for constant affirmation, maladaptive denial of inconvenient or dispiriting truths and realities, and other psychopathological problems. Egotism afflicts the liberal mind.

Mr. Ray soberly concludes one of his recent papers on liberalism by cautioning that though liberals deceive us by their noisy advocacy of democratic principles, "Leftism IS intrinsically authoritarian and power-loving and will always therefore tend in the direction of government domination" and will succeed only if not impeded by other forces and influences. And given the opportunity which comes from political power, Leftists, true to form, will quickly expand their power by fashioning oppressive bureaucracies to facilitate their socialist and collectivist goals. (And, yes, folks, that expansion is already taking place at breakneck speed. Do the Dept. of Education, EPA and other suffocating regulatory bodies come to mind?)

He also asserts that to Leftists constitutional constraints are but inconvenient hurdles to be either circumvented or overwhelmed. (Strict Constitutional constructionists and originalists they surely aren't.) "Giving any power to Leftists is a most dangerous thing to do," Ray warns, "and working to prevent that happening is a matter of no small importance."

Finally, when recently speaking with two professional acquaintances, one a Volunteer Coordinator with a major non-profit and the other a military retiree, I was at once mystified and distressed by what clearly appeared to be their unwavering view that since most Americans had already irretrievably morphed into permissive and dependent automatons that there was really nothing more that could done, or, indeed, should be done to resist America's socialist transformation. In fact, any commitment to action on their part to restore and defend American exceptionalism seemed to be altogether absent or, at best, tentative. I couldn't help but think that these otherwise regular folks had simply given up hope and resigned themselves to quietly and willingly succumb to the new Progressive order, much like the sleeping human victims of the alien pods in "Invaders from Space" were transformed into emotionless alien clones.

Thus, while their words seemed to express their disappointment over the country's direction, they seemed strangely resigned to a fate over which they felt they could not or, worse, did not want to exercise any meaningful level of control. I remained bewildered by their alarming unwillingness to remedy the situation by their own political engagement and activism. Very disturbing, indeed.

I can only hope and pray that these folks are not typical of most Americans, for if they are America is surely doomed. And I guess this is why I'm a stalwart Conservative, aka Classical Liberal: I want to protect my individual rights and liberties from an overreaching authority no matter what form that authority may take. And as a grassroots activist, I am completely unwilling to resign myself to a socialist or fascist fate.

Finally, what this research has taught me is that yielding to, compromising with or in any way accommodating Modern Liberalism merely to achieve some semblance of transitory peace is foolhardy, suicidal and simply irrational. Tough love, pushing back deliberately and firmly, refusing to back off, and not simply emotionally reacting to their adolescent and self-destructive behavior is the tried and true course to follow. Thus, it appears that patriots and parents really do have much in common.

So let's roll, America! And don't for a moment allow them to get the best of us, or, more importantly, our Republic.

("The roots of liberalism – and its associated madness – can be clearly identified by understanding how children develop from infancy to adulthood and how distorted development produces the irrational beliefs of the liberal mind; when the modern liberal mind whines about imaginary victims, rages against imaginary villains and seeks above all else to run the lives of persons competent to run their own lives, the neurosis of the liberal mind becomes painfully obvious." Dr. Lyle Rossiter, "The Liberal Mind")

Progressives, aka Democratic Socialists: the Enemy Within (10/2009)

Ever wonder just who's behind the curtains pulling the levers of power in D.C.? Me too. So, I did a little checking and this, in a nutshell, is what I've come up with.

Too often we differentiate our so-called representatives as either Democrat or Republican, liberal or conservative. Then there are the self-described "moderates" on both sides of the aisle who represent…well…themselves and their political careers, which describes the majority of lawmakers on the Hill and in our state legislatures.

But, political party labels aside, who are really the movers and shakers among those who effectively dominate the legislative agenda and, in turn, "we the people"?

The Progressives! To my way of thinking, Democrats-in-name-only (DINOs) are a party unto themselves and a political association completely wedded to a thoroughly alien ideological agenda. Republicans-in-name-only are little better.

Founded in 1991 by Reps Dellums (D-CA), Lane (D-IL), DeFazio (D-OR), Waters (D-CA) and Bernie Sanders (D-VT), the latter now a Senator and the only openly Socialist serving in Congress, the 70 members of the Congressional Progressive Caucus, aka DINOs, espouse Socialism and the agenda of the Democratic Socialists of America. (Estimates run as high as 82 in both Congress and the Senate.)

At one time, Progressives concealed their association with the DSA, an affiliate of the Socialist Internationale, and in circa 2000 their names were scrubbed from the DSA website. In their "Elections Statement 2000", the DSA website noted that "DSA recognizes that some insurgent politicians representing labor, environmentalists, gays and lesbians, and communities of color may choose to run under Democratic auspices…" Love the term "insurgent". It's so…counter-revolutionary. So… frappe. So…in. And, hey, why expose your true ideology to public scrutiny when it might be a political liability?

Unquestionably, the once venerable Democratic Party, of which I was once a proud member, has demonstrably moved radically far left. For all practical purposes, the party is now dominated by those whom the Dems themselves had once derisively labeled "fringe" and "extreme". Well, not any more. On the ascendancy, Progressives are brazenly open about their association with the DSA.

The Progressive Caucus is comprised of often well-positioned power brokers in DC whose essentially uncontested rule continues to influence the course of our republic.

In ruthless pursuit of socialist/collectivist goals, their legislative agenda is relentlessly aimed at effectively transforming the meaning and relevance of the Constitution itself. In short, folks, the Progressive Caucus is a clear and present danger to all Americans of every political stripe who value the Constitution and the Bill of Rights. The damage they have wrought on this nation is nearly incalculable.

In the Progressive Caucus statement of purpose, you can check for yourself some of the code words which reveal their real political ideology and purpose:

"The Progressive Caucus is organized around the principles of social and economic justice...which represent the interests of all people, not just the wealthy and powerful.

...Our people-based agenda extends from job creation to job training, to economic conversion, to single payer healthcare reform, to environmental reform and to women's rights.

...Now that the cold war is over, this nation's budget and overall priorities must reflect that reality. We support further cuts in outdated and unnecessary military spending, a more progressive tax system in which wealthy taxpayers and corporations contribute their fair share, and a substantial increase in social programs for low and middle-income American families."

To accomplish their collectivist goals, their legislative initiatives are invariably aimed at media control (to achieve "fairness", of course);

controlled education (to shape a collectivist viewpoint); the watering down of free speech (to eliminate a free flow of opinions and to shut down debate); disarmament of the citizenry (to eliminate the possibility of armed resistance); legalization of same-sex marriage (to undermine the family); pushing "wage" laws; increasing welfare spending (to buy votes and quell political resistance); eliminating basic voter ID requirements; and advancing global governance. And this is but a smattering of the insanely sophomoric, elitist and dangerous ambitions of the Caucus and of both their minions and unwitting enablers on both sides of the aisle.

In 2005, the Caucus drafted its "Progressive Promise" document (I call it their "manifesto") advocating, among other things, socialized medicine, radical environmentalism, redistribution of wealth, higher taxes, reductions in the government's intelligence gathering capabilities, debt relief for poor countries, and, of course, the precipitous withdrawal of US troops from Iraq & Afghanistan.

The lofty rationale for pursuing these socialist aims? "To re-build US alliances, restore international respect for American power and influence, and to reaffirm our nation's constructive engagement in the United Nations and other multilateral organizations." Sounds eerily like Obama's globalist and socialist pitch, huh? You betcha' it does.

Just so you know who the enemy within really is, as of 2009 the following members of Congress were declared members of the Congressional Progressive Caucus. "Former member" Nancy Pelosi is not a declared member. Also not included are Sen. Brown (D-FL), Sen. Tom Udall (D-MN) and Sen. Bernie Sanders (I-VT) who, by virtue of their being Senators, are no longer members of the Congressional Progressive Caucus:

Neil Abercrombie (D-HI)
Tammy Baldwin (D-WI)
Xavier Becerra (D-CA)
Earl Blumenauer (D-OR)
Bob Brady (D-PA)
Michael Capuano (D-MA)
Andre Carson (C-IN)
Donna Christensen (Virgin Islands)
Judy Chu (D-CA)

Yvette Clarke (D-NY)
William "Lacy" Clay (D-MO)
Emanuel Cleaver (D-MO)
Steve Cohen (D-TN)
John Conyers (D-MI)
Elijah Cummings (D-MD)
Danny Davis (D-IL)
Peter DeFazio (D-OR)
Rosa DeLauro
Donna Edwards (D-MD)
Keith Ellison (D-MN)
Sam Farr (D-CA)
Chaka Fattah (D-PA)
Bob Filner (D-CA)
Barney Frank (D-MA)
Marcia Fudge (D-OH)
Alan Grayson (D-FL)
Raul Grijalva (D-AZ)
Luis Gutierrez (D-IL)
John Hall (D-NY)
Phil Hare (D-IL)
Alcee Hastings (D-FL)
Maurice Hinchey (D-NY)
Mazie Horono (D-HI)
Michael Honda (D-CA)
Jesse Jackson, Jr.
Sheila Jackson-Lee (D-TX)
Eddie Bernice Johnson (D-TX)
Hank Johnson (D-GA)
Marcy Kaptur (D-OH)
Carolyn Kilpatrick (D-MI)
Dennis Kucinich (D-OH)
Dave Loebsack (D-IA)
Barbara Lee (D-CA)
John Lewis (D-GA)
Ben Lujan (D_NM)
Carolyn Maloney (D-NY)
Ed Markey (D-MA)
Eric Massa (D-NY)

Jim McDermott (D-WA)
James P. McGovern (D-MA)
George Miller (D-CA)
Glenn Moore (D-WI)
Jim Moran (D-VA)
Jerrold Nadler (D-NY)
Eleanor Holmes Norton (District of Columbia)
John Oliver (D-MA)
Frank Pallone (D-NJ)
Ed Pastor (D-AZ)
Donald Payne (D-NJ)
Minority Leader. Sure.)
Chellie Pingree (D-ME)
Jared Polis (D-CO)
Charles Rangel (D-NY)
Laura Richardson (D-CA)
Lucille Roybal-Allard (D-CA)
Bobby Rush (D-IL)
Linda Sanchez (D-CA)
Bernie Sanders (I-VT)
Jan Schakowsky (D-IL)
Jose Serrano (D-NY)
Louise Slaughter (D-NY)
Pete Stark (D-CA)
Bennie Thompson (D-MS)
John Tierney (D-MA)
Nydia Velazquez (D-NY)
Maxine Waters (D-CA)
Diane Watson (D-CA)
Mel Watt (D-NC)
Henry Waxman (D-CA)
Peter Welch (D-VT)
Robert Wexler (D-FL)
Lynn Woolsey (D-CA)

For a current list, go to the DSA website.

Supporting the efforts of the Progressive Caucus are such charming organizations as the Institute for Policy Studies, MoveOn.org, ACLU,

Peace Action, Americans for Democratic Action, Progressive Democrats of America, NAACP, League of United Latin American Citizens, Rainbow/PUSH Coalition, National Council of La Raza, Hip Hop Caucus, etc. Don't these names just positively ooze of patriotism and traditional American values? Just gives me goose bumps all over.

So, watch out, folks. These guys are playing for keeps. Our opinions and our Constitution are absolutely irrelevant to them. And the list above doesn't even include a number of Senators, some of whom while not members, are most certainly cut from the same neo-Marxist cloth. You can probably name them faster than I can type them.

As Norman Thomas, Socialist Party of America, observed circa 1925, *"The American people will never knowingly adopt Socialism. But under the name of liberalism they will adopt every fragment of the Socialist program, until one day America will be a Socialist nation without knowing what happened."*

LET'S NOT ALLOW THEM TO GET AWAY WITH THIS SUBTERFUGE. Knowledge is power if we exercise that power. When the time comes, I urge you to volunteer to knock on doors to deny office to any Progressive politician. ANY! If they appear on the membership list of the Democratic Socialists of America, they DON'T belong in a government of the people, by the people and for the people. Expose them!!

Just Who Are the Domestic Terrorists? (02/2012)

It's been reported that in a recent memo to all law enforcement agencies, the FBI counter-terrorism unit associated those who referenced "Constitution", "the Bible", "US Supreme Court decisions", and "treaties with foreign governments" as part of a "domestic terrorist movement". You just can't make this stuff up, folks.

You may recall that in 2009, Homeland Security issued a report on "Right Wing Extremism" labeling those who used terms like "Constitutionalist", "Patriot" or "linking their belief system to the [ideals of the]American Revolution" were also potential national security threats. And, yes, lumped in with these threatening domestic elements were returning American veterans. Folks, this is beyond stupid and offensive. This is scary.

Of course, the Occupy Wall Street and Black Lives Matter "useful idiots", the darlings of the radical left, Soros, Barack Obama and Nancy Pelosi, are nothing but grassroots, highly principled moral paragons of American virtue who are merely trying to peacefully right fundamental wrongs in our depraved capitalist and racist society. Right? But, how do our Progressive overseers explain the hundreds of OWS arrests for violence, trespassing, attacks on policemen, and the wanton destruction of private and public property? Well, they don't explain because no one is making them accountable. Remind you of the formative years of the Nazi movement? It should.

But, nothing to see here, folks. Just move on.

But, just so the FBI and Homeland Security don't miss me on their intrusive radar: **I love the Constitution and am sworn to defend it on my life. I am a Veteran, a Tea Partier and a Patriot to boot. Opponent of a Progressive Utopian America, you betcha'. Defender of our Founders' America, absolutely on my life!**

Notwithstanding Obama's ceaseless attacks on the freedom of religion, add to all this the Administration's relentless assault on our 2nd Amendment rights by its "Fast & Furious" gangsters, aka their so-called "Dept. of Justice", the Democrats' open support of the Occupy Wall Street thugs, both the Democratic Socialist Party's and the American Communist

Party's OPEN support for Obama and his Progressive minions, and Obama's insidious class warfare strategy to pit Americans against Americans, races against races, economic "classes" against economic "classes", and we have a powder keg on our hands. Could that be Obama's intention? To the clear-eyed among us, and at the risk of being politically incorrect, it sure as hell looks that way to me.

On top of this, for some time now I have been monitoring the globalist efforts of Obama's Progressive handmaiden, former Sec. of State Hillary Clinton and likely presidential candidate in 2016, who has been quietly pushing the following loathsome treaties which she hopes Obama will shove down the Senate's throat, a chamber, by the way, currently dominated by Progressives who share Hillary's and Barack's alien globalist goals.

And here are those damnable treaties:

1) the authority of the **International Criminal Court** would be expanded by adding a new crime, that being "aggression", which, in effect, is waging war without the United Nation's approval. This would empower the International Court to prosecute Americans who have not violated any American laws and would give Russia and China veto power over US military actions. (There goes American sovereignty, which is, of course, the globalist goal of these treasonous vermin.)

2) The **Law of the Sea Treaty** (LOST for short): requires that the US contribute half its royalties from offshore drilling to an international entity of 160 members and would allow that body a free hand to distribute those funds in any manner and to any nation they please. The US would be out-numbered 1- 160. Without compensation, LOST would also obligate the US to share its offshore drilling technology with any other nation who asks for it. (Leveling the playing field and redistributing wealth on a global basis.)

3) **Small-Arms Control**: in the work for some time now, Clinton was negotiating a treaty which would require that each signatore to this treaty implement domestic measures to stop the exportation of all small arms and to register all ammunition in order to track its

source. (If Fast & Furious fails to undermine our 2nd Amendment, then this invasive Small Arms Control Treaty will. These statists never give up.)

4) **Outer Space Code of Conduct**: this code would ban activities which are likely to generate debris in outer space. On the surface, EU-endorsed effort is an innocuous international anti-litter campaign in space. How very, very green. HOWEVER, this could very easily lead to prohibiting America's deployment of anti-missile platforms in space. (Not a good idea.)

5) **Rights of the Child**: And just who wouldn't support the rights of children? But at the needless risk of jeopardizing our sovereignty, Comrade Clinton was pushing for the establishment of a 14-member court which would oversee the international distribution of funds for shelter, food clothing and education for children in poor nations. This could mean that the court would be able to successfully challenge the United States if, in the court's opinion, Americans weren't forking over enough. (Totally unnecessary and inane.) The United States Agency for International Development doesn't need to be told how to distribute America's foreign aid. Again, a Progressive attack on our sovereignty.)

The disturbing reality is that America's sovereignty, our freedom, our liberties, our Constitution, our constitutional republic are of little consequence to the self-serving and shortsighted Progressive ideologues now ruling our lives and transforming our republic out of existence.

And if I hear one more time how much better off the country would be with Hillary rather than Barry at the helm, I will implode! Destructive of our way of life and disloyal alien-oriented fruitcakes of the first order, these Progressives must be STOPPED!

On the treaty issue, I recommend that readers pass this list on to their congresspersons, Senators, the Senate Minority Leader and the Speaker of House. Tell them NOT to allow the further undermining of either our Constitution or our sovereignty by the Senate's misguided passage of these outrageously offensive treaties.

So, if the goal of terrorism is to instill fear, disorder and instability in order to facilitate fundamental political change, and aside from some imported and homegrown conniving Jihadists and a handful of weirdo "militia" groups, who else among us is a clear and present danger to our families and communities, our liberties and our God-given right to pursue happiness? Now think hard. I'm sure you'll get it. No fair peeking!

Yup! You got it. The PROGRESSIVES! Dangerous to a person, these unprincipled vermin now dominate the once venerable Democratic Party and infect many in the Republican rank and file as well. We call them RINOs. So, don't be fooled by "Democrat" or "Republican" labels. It's well past time to call a spade a spade and to hold these brigands accountable for their faithlessness and treachery.

[3] CONSTITUTIONAL ISSUES

A Quick Look at Original Intent (3/2011)

Rather than routinely adding more of my opinions to the millions already ignored out there, over the past year I have been slowly diverting more of my focus to better understanding the original meaning of the Constitution, the very pillar of our experiment in republicanism.

As a result of that effort, I have come to appreciate that only with a clearer, uncorrupted understanding of our guiding principles can we more easily distinguish revisionist interpretations from those which fully comport with our founders' meaning and intent.

Frankly, since taking this self-help tack, I have, sadly, discovered a mountain of disinformation and misrepresentation in the news media and blogosphere alike.

Some of our own politicians--especially on the left--who have taken the oath to preserve, protect and defend the Constitution are among the worst offenders. Whether it is deliberate or simply born of ignorance, the revisionism emanating from all levels of government and media is truly breathtaking and a serious threat to our Republic.

To help me understand these countless misrepresentations of our Constitution, I've taken the time to research and to briefly write about the "Commerce Clause", "Necessary and Proper Clause", the "Supremacy Clause", the 2nd and 10th Amendments, Term Limits and Judicial Review. Tackling these intensely interesting topics has broadened my understanding of our founders' intent and meaning and has, I believe, made me a more responsible and critically thinking citizen. Though it's only a start, I have at least now been able to delight in making it harder for revisionists—both on the left and the right--to get away with their arrogant misrepresentations.

This time, I'm very briefly tackling the principle of "original intent", what it means and how we determine what it is. Caution: this is only introductory and most certainly not intended to be a comprehensive treatment of the subject. But, like I said, it's a start, and I hope it's helpful to the reader as well.

As noted in previous posts, the principle of "judicial review" has long ago given way to "judicial activism", "judicial revisionism" and, today, relatively unbridled "judicial supremacy". Among too many jurists today, familiarity with case law alone and a proclivity for advancing political and social engineering agendas has, in whole or in part, supplanted their fidelity to the Constitution.

In the words of Thomas Jefferson, the Supreme Court and its appellate network have evolved into a "judicial oligarchy", quite at odds with their original role as "faithful guardians of the Constitution" and woefully incompatible with the bedrock principle of constitutional supremacy.

So, just how do we determine original intent and meaning, this to prevent our further straying from the founders' republican plan of governance? And how do we detect misrepresentations?

In his book, "Original Intent", David Barton lists10 tactics which "historical revisionists" continue to routinely employ in order to misrepresent history and to misinterpret the Constitution in order to advance their political agendas. And while none of these tactics will surprise the reader, these disreputable and thoroughly unprincipled practices bear repeating here: "the use of patent untruths; overly broad generalizations; outright omissions/misquotations; insinuations and innuendos; impugning morality; presenting fiction as though it were fact; the use of psychohistory/psychobabble; failure to account for etymology (changes in the meanings of words); and the absence of primary source references." More than I want to get into here, but very well-worth perusing in Chapter 16 of his book.

In "The Original Constitution", Robert Natelson assures us that "we can reconstruct most of the original Constitution's meaning with clarity and confidence" if we become familiar with period historical records and 1787 law. More specifically, he tells us we should familiarize ourselves with the words of both the *framers* and the *ratifiers* which he respectively refers to as the Constitution's *drafters* and *makers*, and to rely on Bacon's *Abridgment* or Jacob's *New Law Dictionary* to capture the actual and prevailing meanings of their words.

The drafters (framers), 55 in number, wrote and explained the document to the 1,648 state ratifiers (makers) who, based upon the latter's understanding of the document as explained to them by the framers, adopted it, Rhode Island being the last state to ratify the Constitution in May 1790. Thus, how ratifying conventions (the makers), representing "we the people" in the several states, understood the intent and meaning of the Constitution as explained to them by the framers is referred to as "original understanding" and is, of course, centrally important to our understanding the Constitution. (Re-read this paragraph and let it sink in.)

Natelson tells us to bear in mind that undergirding the Constitution are these guiding principles with which all founders, both framers and ratifiers alike, were in agreement: <u>liberty, natural/unalienable rights of individuals;</u> <u>effective, decentralized, limited, republican (responsible to the people)</u> <u>government; fiduciary government (meaning a government acting in good</u> <u>faith and honestly on behalf of the people).</u> And always remember that intent and meaning are predicated upon these inviolable principles.

Within the context of 1787 law and the prevailing rules of legal interpretation, the founders agreed that *"to properly construe original meaning one would need to construe the meaning as a reasonable and involved person at the time and under those conditions peculiar to that moment would have done so,"* relying heavily on how the ratifiers/makers—NOT the framers/drafters—interpreted the meaning.

Why the heavier reliance upon the ratifiers' understanding? How supportive the state ratifiers were of adopting the Constitution hinged

upon their own understanding of the document as presented and
explained to them by the framers whose challenging and single-minded
task it was to persuade the States to join the new-found republican
union. Thus, <u>the ratifiers' understanding of the Constitution is absolutely</u>
<u>essential to achieving "original understanding".</u>

Also, to accurately construe meaning, scholars rely upon the principle
of "equitable construction", meaning that when a document's wording
appears to conflict with the intent of the framers, that the latter, that
being <u>the INTENT, once correctly and objectively deduced, holds sway.</u>
Obviously, this requires considerable due diligence and no small amount
of intellectual integrity.

Then there's the rule of construction known as "designatio unius est
exclusio alterius'" (naming one thing implies the exclusion of the other)
which is a time-honored means of construing the makers' intent. In his
book, Barton clearly illustrates this rule with this example: if your wife
tells you to pick up lettuce, tomatoes, and onions at the store, this means
to the exclusion of celery and pudding. (Very importantly, this also means
that 'enumerated powers" are just that—inclusive only of those expressed
powers and exclusive of all others.)

Most critically, when exercising any of the rules of construction, it must
be accompanied by objectivity and judgment and, again, the exercise
must be purposefully aimed at accurately exposing the makers' intent, and
not of advancing one's personal political predilections—surely a very tall
order and, for many jurists, lawyers and politicians today, an apparently
insuperable and superhuman task.

Henry Monaghan, in "Our Perfect Constitution", warned that <u>attorneys</u>
<u>and jurists, often without an adequate historical perspective, tend to</u>
<u>"subordinate good facts to a good argument", all in an effort to coax a</u>
<u>faulty meaning from the Constitution merely in order to win their case</u>
<u>or argument.</u> This, of course, can lead to corrupted case law and specious
precedents upon which subsequent rulings are erroneously based. So
much for the incorruptibility of case law and the misplaced glory and
overblown sacrosanctity of *stare decisis*. (Nothing like piling error on
error, huh?)

In the absence of ratifying documentation as in the case of Delaware, New Jersey and Georgia, each of which fairly quickly adopted the Constitution with little discussion, one must remember that the Federalist framers normally went to great lengths to educate, allay the misgivings of, and to win over state ratifiers. They were quintessential marketers and exerted every effort to ensure ratification. Thus, in these particular states where there is a paucity of ratification records, scholars can correctly assume that the framers' explanations accurately reflected these ratifiers' understanding of the framers' meaning and intent. Makes sense.

We should also bear in mind this cautionary note by David Barton: <u>trying to construe original meaning from materials generated *AFTER* full adoption of the Constitution (May 29, 1790) and the Bill of Rights (December 15, 1791) will inevitably lead to error and misinterpretation.</u> (And the litany of revisionist case law since ratification would seem to fully bear that out.)

Underscoring the importance of construing original intent and meaning, and much to the dismay of "living and evolving constitution" adherents, it is vital to recall John Dickinson's words: "We are not forming plans for a Day, Month, Year or Age, but Eternity." In other words, **it is the obligation of judges to keep times in tune with the Constitution, not to keep the Constitution in tune with the times.** (Not sure where I found that quote, but there it is.) Thus, adhering to a so-called "living constitution" approach inherently violates our framers' intent. Thus, only by our dutifully applying the interpretive principles described above can we effectively counteract revisionism and the corrosiveness of a "living constitution" mindset.

Also, as Barton explains in his book, the framers uniformly understood that "judicial review" was necessarily limited to judging the constitutionality of a law against the "<u>specific, self-evident wording</u> of the Constitution itself"—in other words, "constitutional supremacy" should always trump "judicial supremacy". Obviously, that formula has not been dutifully applied in today's world of activist/revisionist jurisprudence.

In Federalist #81, Hamilton noted that "there is not a syllable in the Constitution which directly empowers the national courts to construe the laws according to the *spirit* of the Constitution." And James Kent similarly explained that the Judiciary could compare a law only to "the *true intent* and *meaning* of the Constitution," the abiding concern of the framers being that if the judges were allowed the latitude of interpreting the more ethereal meaning, aka "spirit", of the Constitution "they risked imputing any meaning they might personally desire in order to reflect their own prejudices and values." (Thus, having heretofore often insisted that true patriots should dutifully and carefully abide by the *spirit*, meaning and intent of the Constitution, I now stand corrected. It is now clear that to objectively and accurately deduce the original meaning and intent of the Constitution, divining the *spirit* of the Constitution should be left to the clairvoyant. Lesson learned. Thank you, Mr. Hamilton.)

Unsurprisingly, the framers specifically forbade the judiciary becoming policy-makers or legislators. To wit, framer Rufus King warned that "judges must interpret the laws; they ought not to be legislators", thus eclipsing the power of Congress. To the framers, the unsettling outcome of such judicial overreach would be public disorder and possible disintegration of the union itself. In fact, Jefferson warned "that the dissolution of our federal government is in the constitution of the federal judiciary; ...working like gravity at night and by day, gaining a little today and a little tomorrow, and advancing its noiseless step like a thief, over the field of jurisdiction, until all shall be usurped." Prophetic.

Obviously, that is where we are today. And though Jefferson held that the people are the ultimate authority in our republican system of governance, David Barton soberly observed that "today the so-called 'tyranny of the majority' has [now] been replaced by the 'tyranny of the minority'", referencing many instances of majority electoral rulings being imperiously overturned by activist courts, something never, ever dreamed of or intended by the founders. (The court's overturning California voters on the issue of gay marriage is an instructive example of serious judicial lawlessness.) To underscore his point, Barton went on to say that "a foreign observer in modern America today would likely conclude that the President and Congress have taken oaths to uphold the Court's opinion of the Constitution." Heck, most Americans have come to share that view as well. And, of course, it is this sorry state of affairs which must be remedied if our carefully crafted of-for-and-by-the-people Republic is to survive. When we grant supremacy to a corruptible ruling elite we violate original intent and expose ourselves to tyranny.

Since each branch of government is enjoined to uphold the Constitution as the supreme law of the land, and bearing in mind that each branch of government is inherently empowered by the framers to exercise judicial review, framer James Wilson asserted that the President can "refuse to carry into effect an act that violates the Constitution." So too Congress. <u>So too the States, the immediate fiduciary representatives of the people.</u>

Jefferson noted that "both magistracies [Executive and Judicial branches] are equally independent in the sphere of action assigned to them."

And with respect to Congress, framer Luther Martin declared <u>"a knowledge of mankind and of legislative affairs cannot be presumed to belong in a higher degree to the Judges than to the Constitution."</u> Jefferson further explained that "each of the three departments has equally the right to decide for itself what its duty is under the Constitution without any regard to what others may have decided for themselves under a similar question." Point: <u>the Constitution and "we the people", not the Judiciary nor any other branch or level of government, constitute the supreme law of the land. When government laws, edicts, rulings violate the people's understanding of the Constitution, those acts are null and void.</u> (Note: this underscores the applicability and constitutional authority of both the 9th and 10th Amendments.)

Thus, a fundamental truth none of us should forget is that the founders rejected the notion that the judiciary is the final arbiter of what is and is not constitutional. Truth be told, we the people, the ratifiers of the Constitution and the republic we created, are, absolutely and without question, the final arbiters of what is and is not constitutional. Never, EVER forget that.

More to the point, Lincoln asserted that "if the policy of the whole government is to be fixed by decision of the Supreme Court,...the people will have ceased to be their own masters" which, of course dovetails with Hamilton's assertion that of the three branches, "the Judiciary is beyond comparison the weakest" which, of course, was by design. Wouldn't know that today though, would you?

Though seemingly self-evident, it's important to note <u>that the Court may rule on the constitutionality of a law, thus "voiding" it, but it cannot</u>

nullify it, that is to say prevent its enforcement. (Andrew Jackson made that clear when he forced Cherokees to move west in defiance of the Supreme Court. To paraphrase Jackson, "Well, they made the ruling. Now let them enforce it.") Also, it is axiomatic that an unconstitutional court ruling is inherently without force. Point: the President and Congress have not taken oaths to uphold the Court's opinion as to what is and is not constitutional. So, in that sense, neither the Courts nor any other branch of the federal government may abrogate or otherwise lawfully ignore the people's will. Ultimate power ultimately resides squarely with the people. Period.

Like other constitutional scholars, Barton counsels that the solution to stemming the disintegration of our republican system of governance is the resurgence of an educated, virtuous electorate which is able and willing to differentiate between candidates of character with fidelity to the Constitution and those who are only loosely attached to basic moral and constitutional principles. He also warned that our pell-mell slide toward democracy, aka "mobocracy", or majority rule on the basis of *feelings* rather than *timeless* Constitutional principles and laws, must be reversed with all deliberate speed or we lose it all.

Noah Webster warned that "when a citizen gives his suffrage (his vote) to a man of known immorality he abuses his trust (civic responsibility); he sacrifices not only his own interest, but that of his neighbor; he betrays the interest of his country." Lesson: we must cast aside our political party-first blinders and allow the clear meaning and intent of the Constitution to inform our viewpoints and our selection of candidates to represent us.

Jefferson warned that "if a nation expects to be ignorant—and free—in a state of civilization, it expects what never was and never will be." Thus, it is incumbent upon each of us to familiarize ourselves and others with original intent.

Chief Justice John Jay counseled that "every member of the State ought diligently to read and to study the constitution of his country...By knowing their rights, they will sooner perceive when they are violated and be the better prepared to defend and assert them." Toward this end, it is crystal clear to me that we should each strive to be thoroughly familiar with the Constitution, never delegating that civic duty to revisionists, scholarly though they may appear to be, or to attorneys who have been schooled in case law rather than the clear meaning and intent of the Constitution itself.

Again, though it requires some level of diligence on our part, understanding the Constitution is NOT rocket science. Why? Because the framers never intended it to be so. It's a relatively straightforward document, the people's guide to republican governance.

Samuel Adams warned that "a state of indolence, inattention and security... is forever the forerunner of slavery."

Daniel Webster cautioned that "I apprehend no danger to our country from a foreign foe...Our destruction, should it come at all, will be...from the inattention of the people to the concerns of their government, from their carelessness and negligence."

Finally, Pres. Garfield counseled that "...the people are responsible for the character of their Congress. **If that body be ignorant, reckless, and corrupt, it is because the people tolerate [it].**" Wow! He certainly has aptly described the horrifically unpleasant state of political affairs in which we find ourselves today. Some of the asinine, dismissive and ignorant statements about the Constitution uttered by some of our DC reps have been particularly unsettling and offensive.

Ultimately then, folks, the fate of our constitutional republic and our individual liberties rests squarely upon our willingness to actively and knowledgeably participate in our political process, and to insist that our representatives remain faithful to the Constitution. And, frankly, save for the Tea Party and Nullification Movements today, we've been blowing it big time.

The "Commerce Clause", "Necessary & Proper Clause" and Obamacare

Having culled through reams of often esoteric judicial analyses and rulings since ratification of the Constitution in 1787, the inescapable conclusion is that over the years the Supreme Court, Congress and the Executive have egregiously misinterpreted and progressively broadened the original and intentionally narrow meaning the Framers attached to both the Commerce Clause and the Necessary & Proper Clause. And therein lies the problem: liberal misinterpretation of these clauses has served to extend federal jurisdiction and control far beyond the Framers' original intent.

Obamacare's "individual mandate" has once again put Art 1, Sec 8, Clause 3, the Commerce Clause, front and center. And like all things Constitutional these days, even a casual observer can readily see that over the years the courts and the politicians have managed to grossly distort--indeed violate--the original meaning and intent of this clause with a litany of tortured legal argumentation and capricious social engineering justifications.

To begin with, the Commerce Clause states that the United States Congress shall have the power *"to regulate Commerce with foreign Nations, and among the several States, and with the Indian Tribes."* Not surprisingly, when linked with Art 1, Sec 8, Clause 18, aka the Necessary and Proper Clause, over the years the federal government has empowered itself to further and irresponsibly expand the original scope of the Commerce Clause

By way of background, as a direct result of the Founders' unsettling experience with the Articles of Confederation, the Framers understood the practical need to better ensure unimpeded uniformity in interstate commerce, that is to say the unencumbered "trade or exchange" of goods among the States, this in order to achieve efficient interstate commercial intercourse free of State-imposed discriminatory and retaliatory restrictions such as duties which if left unchecked could well have led to the collapse of the confederation itself.

As James Madison counseled, "[the federal regulation of commerce] is necessary to preserve the Union, for "without [such regulation], the Union will infallibly crumble to pieces."

Therefore, as nearly as I can deduce this effort to achieve uniformity was intended to reduce, minimize, or altogether eliminate needless and onerous State-mandated barriers and regulations which impeded the free and efficient trade or exchange of goods among the States. Period.

It is important to note that the limits of congressional jurisdiction over interstate commerce may be easily found in Clauses 5 and 9 of Art 1, Sec 9:

Clause 5: "No Tax or Duty shall be laid on Articles exported from any State."

Clause 6: "No Preference shall be given by any Regulation of Commerce or Revenue to the Ports of one State over those of another: nor shall Vessels bound to, or from, one State, be obliged to enter, clear, or pay Duties in another."

Clearly, the emphasis is on *interstate* duties and revenues, not upon the articles/goods traded or produced *within* those States. Thus, as originally understood the power to regulate interstate trade did not mean the authority to prohibit, nor did it in any way imply the power to impose penalties for violations of the Commerce Clause.

Important to note too is that the Necessary and Proper Clause, a clause relentlessly exploited by Progressives over the years, was in no way intended by the Framers to permit the federal government to assume any authority outside its clearly defined enumerated powers in Art 1, Sec 8. To wit, in John Marshall's discussion of *McCulloch v Maryland*, he clearly drew a distinction between the proper definition of "necessary" as meaning "indispensably requisite" versus the improper definition being that of "convenient". In other words, the federal government could not arrogate unto itself any extraordinary implementing power other than that which was clearly "indispensably requisite" in order to execute its clearly defined enumerated powers, in this case to regulate interstate commerce.

But a cursory examination of case law since ratification of the Constitution demonstrates how the proper definition has often been ignored, misconstrued or grossly misinterpreted by an overweening Congress and an enabling gaggle of misguided or politically activist jurists.

Having consulted applicable Federalist papers and *Samuel Johnson's Dictionary of the English Language*, the latter which guided the Framers in their choice and meaning of words, it is obvious that the Constitutional meaning of "commerce" was limited to the trafficking and exchange of goods between the States from one port to another, and not at all to the regulation of INTRAstate production, manufacturing, sale, or the quality of goods/articles; that, therefore, the central and sole purpose of the Commerce Clause was to affirmatively prevent the confusing, conflicting and disorderly imposition of duties among the states. Nothing more.

Even casual examination of founding documents underscores our Framers' clear understanding that "regulate" in 1787 meant "to make regular or normal" or "to remove impediments" to the free flow of interstate commerce. Again, it manifestly did NOT mean federal control or the federal imposition of regulations per se over the INTRAstate production of goods and services.

Significantly, the *US v E.C. Knight Co.* ruling in 1895, aka the *Sugar Trust Case*, instructively asserted the States' sphere of power in matters of commerce thusly:

1. Production is always local, and under the exclusive domain of the States

2. Commerce among the States (interstate commerce) does not begin until goods commence their final movement from their state of origin to that of their destination.

3. The sale of any product is merely an incident of its production and is therefore under the domain of the State because its effect on interstate commerce is merely incidental.

4. Combinations or associations organized for the sale and distribution of goods are under the regulatory power of the State since the effect on interstate commerce is indirect, not direct.

Can't get clearer than that. The ruling upheld and sharply emphasized the core restraints on federal power as intended by the 10th Amendment.

Following passage of the <u>Interstate Commerce Act of 1887</u> which created the Interstate Commerce Commission which was principally intended to check railroad abuse and discrimination, the level of federal usurpation in commerce which ensued was nothing short of mind-boggling--almost laughable if it weren't so utterly unconstitutional. (For example, I learned that the hapless hamburger is now subject to no fewer than 41,000+ State and federal regulations, covering everything from meat production, grazing practices of cattle, conditions in the slaughterhouse, processing methods, sales to retailers, restaurants and fast-food outlets. Ketchup is another example of regulatory overreach: to be considered Grade A, it must flow no more than 9 centimeters in 30 seconds at 69 degrees Fahrenheit. Progressive insanity!)

Though Congress has cited the Commerce Clause to justify Obamacare, logic and an objective analysis of original intent clearly demonstrate that individual mandates, as called for in the healthcare law, are profoundly unconstitutional—PROFOUNDLY! But to myopic and Progressive "living constitution" adherents who care little about the original meaning of the Constitution, or, frankly, the Constitution in any of its original form, Obamacare is nothing more than another harmless *necessary and proper* expansion of the federal government's implied vs enumerated powers. Where are our Founders when they are so sorely needed?!?!?!? Where are our faithful representatives and jurists?!?!?!?!?

With particular respect to Obamacare, I couldn't find one single court ruling in the history of the United States which remotely endorsed the right of the federal government to mandate that every person purchase a product or service or be fined for not doing so. Not one! And though it was difficult to imagine that the Supreme Court could have clear-headedly and in good conscience ruled in favor of this mandate, we cannot forget the corrosive influence of judicial activism and congressional overreach which have passed for rule of law in these United States over the last 100 years. And now that a majority on the Supreme Court has upheld the mandate, Americans must carefully recall and take to heart these words in the Declaration of Independence:

"…But when the long train of abuses and usurpations, pursuing invariably the same object, evinces a design to reduce them under absolute despotism, it is their right, it is their duty, to throw off such government [or abusive power], and to provide new guards for their future security." Amen to that!

So, what's the answer to this unrestrained federal overreach? Very simply, WE must take action to restore the sovereignty of "we the people"!!! Our merely waiting for the next election to throw the bums out and to replace them with what will likely be yet another crop of bums may sound like a solution, but it will accomplish nothing. Inescapably, State nullification action--with teeth--in combination with widespread civil disobedience are most likely the only way to peacefully restore constitutional order. It's now or never...

"...whensoever the General Government assumes undelegated powers, its acts are unauthoritative, void, and of no force; where powers are assumed by the federal government which have not been delegated by the Constitution, a nullification of the act is the rightful remedy." James Madison and Thomas Jefferson, Kentucky and Virginia Resolutions, 1798

"The true key for the construction of everything doubtful in a law is the intention of the law-makers. This is most safely gathered from the words, but may be sought also in extraneous circumstances provided they do not contradict the express words of the law." Thomas Jefferson, letter to Albert Gallatin, 1808

"The court will almost assuredly resort to the great defense shield of denial known as 'stare decisis' as a clever way of protecting the courts own judicial malpractice from scrutiny while at the same time leaving its vast centralization of power in Congress intact." P.A. Madison, Federalist Blog, 2010

"What is to be the consequence, in case the Congress shall misconstrue this part [the necessary and proper clause] of the Constitution and exercise powers not warranted by its true meaning, I answer the same as if they should misconstrue or enlarge any other power vested in them...the success of the usurpation will depend on the executive and judiciary departments, which are to expound and give effect to the legislative acts; and in a last resort a remedy must be obtained from the people, who can by the elections of more faithful representatives, annul the acts of the usurpers." James Madison, Federalist No. 44

POSTSCRIPT:

In 2012, Chief Justice Roberts gratuitously and stunningly ruled that Obamacare's "mandate" was, in fact, a tax, this despite Obama's own attorneys insisting--for purely political reasons--that the mandate was not a tax. By his ruling that the mandate was a tax, the mandate fell within congressional constitutional authority. Doesn't get more twisted, harebrained and lawless than this. Impeachable offense, I'd say.

The Mangled "Supremacy Clause"

For a painfully long time now, the federal government has relied upon a perverted interpretation of the Supremacy Clause to justify its unconstitutional overreach, the imposition of Obamacare in 2010 being among the greatest of its perversions.

Relying upon our Founders' wisdom as expressed in their own words, and upon a few foundational 19th century Supreme Court rulings, in this post I have attempted to very briefly show how extraordinarily flawed modern liberal Supremacy Clause justifications really are.

Article VI, Paragraph 2 (Supremacy Clause); "This Constitution, and the Laws of the United States **which shall be made in Pursuance thereof**; and all Treaties made, or which shall be made, under the Authority of the United States, shall be the supreme Law of the Land; and the Judges in every State shall be bound thereby, any Thing in the Constitution or Laws of any State to the contrary notwithstanding."

The practical purpose of this clause was to eliminate the confusing and often conflicting matrix of State-made and State-threatened treaties with foreign powers which afflicted the union under the Articles of Confederation. Primarily intended to ensure that only the federal government could legally enter into treaties with foreign entities, this clause was uniformly binding upon the States; however, it is important to note in passing that this clause was never intended to accommodate treaties with any foreign entity, e.g. the UN, which would in any way supersede the U.S. Constitution.

Based upon my reading of the Constitution and applicable Federalist Papers, this clause underscored the Founders' belief that when exercising any of the powers *specifically enumerated in the Constitution (per Art 1, Sec 8)* the federal government must prevail over any conflicting or inconsistent State exercise of power, certainly a prudent and practical approach to achieving orderly governance—and an approach ratified by the States.

Further amplifying this meaning, in **McCulloch v Maryland** (1819), Chief Justice Marshall ruled that "the government of the Union, though limited in its power, *is supreme within its sphere of action.*" Thus, the

Supremacy Clause renders federal power supreme only insofar as that power exercised falls within its clearly defined enumerated powers (Art. 1, Sec 8).

An ardent advocate of a strong central government, even James Madison, aka "father of the Constitution", stated that "the proposed [federal] government cannot be deemed a national one, since its jurisdiction extends to certain enumerated objects only, and *leaves to the several States a residuary and inviolable sovereignty over all objects."*

Alexander Hamilton, no less an advocate of a strong central government, warned that "it will not follow from this doctrine (supremacy/preemption) that acts of the large society which are not pursuant to its constitutional powers, but which are invasions of the residuary authorities of the smaller societies, will become the supreme law of the land. *These will be merely acts of usurpation, and will deserve to be treated as such."*

In **Dred Scott v Sandford** (1857), the court ruled that "although the Government of the United States is sovereign and supreme *in its appropriate sphere of action,* yet it does not possess all the powers which usually belong to the sovereignty of a nation. Certain specified powers, enumerated in the Constitution, have been conferred upon it; and *neither the legislative, executive, nor judicial departments of the Government can lawfully exercise any authority beyond the limits marked out by the Constitution."*

In **United States v Reese** (1876), the court ruled that "within its legitimate sphere, Congress is supreme;…but if it steps outside of its constitutional limitations, and attempts that which is beyond its reach, *the courts are authorized to annul its encroachments upon the reserved power of the States and the people."*

The Federalist Blog notes that "if you want to invalidate some State law under the preemption doctrine the burden is on the plaintiff to point to the clause in the United States Constitution that exclusively delegates Congress the authority to make the law, and point to the express prohibition against the States to touch it. Simply having two conflicting laws is not enough; *the burden is on the federal government to show its law is in pursuance of the Constitution* and that it is an area expressly prohibited to the States to act upon, and thus, giving the law national supremacy." For 10th Amendment advocates, understanding this is extremely important.

Fearful of tyrannical federal overreach, John Hancock, Sam Adams, Patrick Henry and George Mason demanded more specificity with respect to the delineation of federal and state powers/jurisdiction. Thus, the Bill of Rights, the first ten amendments to the Constitution, was adopted which explicitly limited powers of the newly formed federal government. To wit, the 9th Amendment states that "the enumeration in the Constitution, of certain rights, shall not be construed to deny or disparage others retained by the people," and the 10th Amendment which states that "the powers not delegated to the United States by the Constitution, nor prohibited by it to the States, are reserved to the States respectively, or to the people". (Note: The Bill of Rights enumerate sacred, inviolable natural God-given rights which the federal government cannot in any way abridge or deny—with or without the Bill of Rights as a shield. The 9th and 10th Amendments merely underscore that these natural rights are absolutely untouchable/inalienable.)

Thus, despite federal attempts to draw upon "necessary and proper" (Art. 1, Sec 8, para 18) justifications for expansively exercising federal authority, *ALL powers not specifically delegated to the federal government reside exclusively with the States and the people.* Though activist jurists have, over the years, made mincemeat of these clear-cut foundational principles, it's really that simple and straightforward. In short, the true intention of the framers is perfectly clear and their words are available for politicians and jurists alike to read.

To either a layman or constitutional scholar, it is crystal-clear that for the federal government to exercise authority by its reliance upon the Supremacy Clause that authority exercised must fully comport with those powers specifically granted to it in the Constitution. And to ensure the integrity of constitutional order, per the 10th Amendment unconstitutional federal laws may not only be properly pre-empted, but MUST be pre-empted/nullified by the states. (Note the Virginia & Kentucky Resolutions of 1798 in which Thomas Jefferson and James Madison defended the right and duty of States to assert their sovereignty by nullifying unconstitutional acts of the federal government.)

Though perverted case law since the Constitutional Convention now suggests otherwise, no amount of judicial revisionism, political expediency or social engineering can lawfully justify our conveniently misinterpreting or willfully concealing the Constitution's original intent and meaning.

My fervent hope is that all case law, like a malignant cancer, which has defiled and deviated from the original intent and meaning of the Constitution over the years will, in time, be excised—sooner rather than later--from the laws of our land. And I pray that this is the unwavering goal of any Article V Convention of States or patriotic platform going forward.

A return to our Constitutional roots is all that can save the Constitution and the exceptional country it has spawned. And it is toward that noble end all Americans must strive lest our Republic, the most vibrant and most successful political experiment in the history of Mankind, is lost forever to ourselves, our progeny and to the world.

("If it be asked, What is the most sacred duty and the greatest source of our security in a Republic? The answer would be, An inviolable respect for the Constitution and Laws--the first growing out of the last...A sacred respect for the constitutional law is the vital principle, the sustaining energy of a free government." Alexander Hamilton, 1794)

("There comes a time in each generation when people must decide whether to stand up and defend their natural rights or bow down before the seat of power. Let us steadfastly maintain our resolve to see this battle through to victory!" John Tate, President, Campaign for Liberty, March 2010)

("Experience has shewn, that even under the best forms of government those entrusted with power have, in time, and by slow operations, perverted it into tyranny." Thomas Jefferson)

The Mangled "Welfare Clause"

For a long time now, the Constitution which our leaders and representatives have sworn to uphold and defend has been routinely violated. As the years go by, the pace and breadth of violations has accelerated and expanded.

Understanding that Congressional overreach has resulted in our country's being saddled with nearly $100+ Trillion in Medicare and Social Security unfunded liabilities alone, there is little doubt that unrestrained federal encroachment and its signature "bread and circuses" profligacy is fast leading this country to insolvency and political dissolution.

Article 1, Section 8 of the Constitution enumerates 18 specific powers granted to Congress. (Note: the original document enumerated 17 powers.) National healthcare, cap and trade, card check, bailouts, pork barrel expenditures and a litany of other legislative initiatives are most certainly not among those legislative powers.

All other powers not specifically granted to Congress in Article 1, Section 8 or in subsequent amendments are, according to the 10th Amendment, reserved solely to the States and to the People.

Clearly, these fundamental elements of the Constitution have been patently ignored or so liberally reinterpreted as to obliterate the original meaning and intent of the framers. It's become painfully obvious that the Progressive stream of legislative abuses which has resulted from the dramatically expansive interpretation of Article 1, Section 8 is leading us to an ideological transformation which is inimical to our founding principles and way of life.

To get us all back onto solid Constitutional footing, in 2013 the **Enumerated Powers Act (HR 450)** was introduced by Rep. Shadegg of Arizona, and was co-sponsored by 48 House members. Very simply, if passed, HR 450/S 1319 would have required Congress to cite the Constitutional authority for each law it offered up for passage. If no constitutional authority clearly existed, the bill couldn't be voted upon or enacted. (To me, this is a perfectly sensible and responsible way to keep Congress more attentive to its pledge to uphold and defend the

Constitution and, yes, to prevent further and avoidable erosion of our Constitution. Frankly, it is inconceivable to me why any conscientious lawmaker wouldn't have been a co-sponsor of the bill or have objected to its passage.)

But, on what basis has so much federal overreach been justified? Further, with passage of HR 450, would we, in fact, once again find ourselves on solid constitutional footing? With these questions in mind, let's ever so very briefly trace the evolution of the meaning and application of the "general welfare and taxation clause".

As alluded to above, the Tenth Amendment provides that "the powers not delegated to the United States by the Constitution, nor prohibited by it to the States, are reserved to the States respectively, or to the people." Thus, one would think there should be, therefore, a reasonably clear and inviolable delineation between federal and State powers. But, as we shall see, that is simply not always so.

The Article 1, Section 8 preamble/clause reads as follows; "The Congress shall have Power to lay and collect Taxes, Duties, Imposts and Excises, to pay the Debts and provide for the common Defence and general Welfare of the United States; but all Duties, Imposts and Excises shall be uniform throughout the United States." This is followed by 17 original enumerated powers.

James Madison, the "father of our Constitution", warned that "if Congress can do whatever in its discretion can be done by money [to] promote the General Welfare, the Government is no longer a limited one, possessing enumerated powers, but an indefinite one, subject to particular exceptions." Accordingly, Madison believed that "promoting the...general welfare" authorized Congress to spend money, but ONLY to carry out the 17 powers and duties specifically and originally enumerated in Article 1, Section 8. (Note again that in the original text, the "welfare clause" was considered by Madison as but a qualifier, a preamble to, but NOT a discrete power unto itself.)

Madison went on to explain that "Congress has not unlimited powers to provide for the general welfare, but to those specifically enumerated; and that, as it was never meant they should raise money for purposes which the enumeration did not place under their action; consequently, that the specification of powers is a limitation of the purposes for which they may raise money." In effect, Madison posited that "I have always regarded [the words] *general welfare* as qualified by the detail of powers (enumerated in Article 1, Section 8) connected to them. *To take them in a literal and unlimited sense would be a metamorphosis of the Constitution not contemplated by its creators.*"

Thomas Jefferson explained it this way: "The laying of taxes is the *power*, and the general welfare the *purpose* for which the power is to be exercised. Congress is not to lay taxes *ad libitum* for any purpose they please; but only to pay the debts or provide for the welfare of the Union. In like manner, they are not to do anything they please to provide for the general welfare, but only to lay taxes for that purpose. To consider the latter phrase, not as describing the purpose of the first, but as giving a distinct and independent power to do any act they please, which might be for the good of the Union, would render all the preceding and subsequent enumerations of power completely useless. *It is an established rule of construction where a phrase will bear either of two meanings, to give it that which will allow some meaning to the other parts of the instrument, and not that which would render all the others useless.*"

Under the Articles of Confederation during and immediately following the Revolution, the central government could raise naval forces and requisition ground forces, but it could not impose taxes or duties to implement those activities unless the States consented. Therein lay the Articles' greatest weakness and the Constitutional Convention was determined not to make that same mistake again. Thus, the enumerated powers of Article 1, Section 8 and the means to execute those powers was included in the Constitution.

While Madison's and Jefferson's meaning of general welfare held sway in the early years of the Republic, in *McCulloch vs Maryland* (1819) Chief Justice Marshall championed the broader Hamiltonian view that the happiness and prosperity of the nation requires not only that the general government has ample powers to effectively ensure the general welfare, but that it has ample means for executing those enumerated powers.

Fast-forward to 1936 when the Supreme Court in an FDR-driven opinion (*US vs Butler*) held that the "general welfare clause granted Congress power it might not derive anywhere else [in the Constitution], but limited the power to spending for matters affecting only the national welfare." It further held that the "general welfare clause confers a power separate and distinct from those 17 powers later enumerated and is not restricted in meaning by the grant of them..." Thus, by legal fiat—and not by constitutional amendment--the number of enumerated powers magically increased from 17 to 18.

Later, in *Helvering vs Davis* (1937), the court rendered a more expansive interpretation by conferring upon Congress power to impose taxes and to spend money for the general welfare subject almost exclusively to its own discretion.

Since then, the more expansive Hamiltonian interpretation which incorporates the preamble into the enumeration of powers has shaped legislative and Supreme Court thinking. (However, here it is worth noting that even to Hamilton pork barrel projects for specific localities exceeded congressional authority. To wit, "the object to which an appropriation of money is to be made [must] be general and not local; its operation extending in fact, or by possibility, throughout the Union, and not being confined to a particular spot.") So, if nothing else, HR 450 would have at least halted the self-serving and costly epidemic of pork barrel spending.

To further muddy the waters, the changing meaning of the word "welfare" itself contributes to the confusion. For instance, in 1828, Webster's dictionary links welfare to protection (from unusual evil or calamity) and security (peace and prosperity). In stark contrast to this earlier definition, however, the current definition is as follows: "aid in the form of money or necessities for those in need; an agency or program through which such aid is distributed." Mindful of the striking contrast and the impact of that contrast to governance, Noah Webster himself posited that *"in the lapse of two or three centuries, changes have taken place which...obscure the sense of the original language; whenever words are understood in a sense different from that which they had when introduced...mistakes may be very injurious."* No kidding.

Theodore Sky, Catholic University School of Law, notes that the expansive interpretation of the enumerated powers has led to an essentially "unbounded modern welfare state." And that's clearly where we now find ourselves as a nation.

So, even with passage of HR 450 and its companion S 1319 in the Senate, continued congressional reliance upon an already expansive interpretation of the general welfare clause will surely render further legislative abuse inevitable. Ultimately, therefore, <u>the only solution might well be a Constitutional amendment which would return Article 1, Section 8 to its original and more restrictive meaning and intent.</u> But, can we hold our collective breath until that happens? Probably not.

Nonetheless, HR 450/S 1319 was a step in the right direction, and, at the very least, the unconstitutional expenditure of billions of dollars for "pork" could finally have been thwarted. That alone should have rendered passage of the Enumerated Powers Act a top priority in D.C.

POSTSCRIPT:

Both HR450 and S1319 died in committee. Gee. Why aren't I surprised?

Executive Orders & the Death of the Republic (10/2012)

Retroactive from 1862, and not until 1907, were Executive Orders (EO's) published in the Federal Register. And today, over 13,000 EO's have been issued and published. But, just what are they, and, more importantly, are they constitutional?

The short of it is that EO's, aka signing statements, presidential determinations, presidential memorandums, presidential notices, presidential orders, have inexorably led to legally binding presidential directives substantially affecting not only executive administrative matters, but both national and foreign policy as well.

With that in mind, the greatest fear of the founders was the establishment of a powerful central government and a strong political leader at the center of that government. They were determined to prevent the rise of monarchs, potentates or czars. Their plan was for a voluntary association of sovereign States in which power emanated from the States and the People, not from an overweening central authority. For the framers and ratifiers, Congress, properly checked by both the Judiciary and the Executive, was intended to be THE focus of federal power and THE source of federal law.

Art I, Sec 1 of the US Constitution concisely and unambiguously provides that "**all** legislative powers herein granted shall be vested in a Congress..." In sharp contrast, Art II specifically outlines Executive powers and duties, none of which include legislating in any form. And to checkmate an overreaching Chief Executive, Art II also provides for the impeachment and removal of not only the Chief Executive, but of any and all officers comprising the Executive Branch.

Originally intended to solely direct executive departments how to faithfully implement laws legislated by Congress, *since the early 20th century EO's have morphed into far-reaching imperial edicts which have little real hope of being invalidated by an unaccountable Supreme Court or overridden by a permissive and faithless Congress.* In fact, in all our history only two EO's have been successfully invalidated/overridden: Truman's 1952 order to place all steel mills under federal control was invalidated by the Supreme Court, and a Clinton EO in 1995 which attempted to prevent the federal government from contracting with organizations that had strike-breakers on the payroll was overturned by Congress. Thus, despite their being in flagrant violation of the Constitution, while EO's can be voided, to do so is, indeed, acutely challenging and, therefore, rarely accomplished.

Worth noting are those less appealing and unsavory EO's such as Franklin Roosevelt's order to remove all Japanese and German Americans from military zones, and to relocate Japanese Americans to internment camps which proceeded unchallenged by either Congress or the Supreme Court. Ya' stray from the Constitution and innocent people DO get hurt.

So, how can Congress void an EO, assuming Congress were so inclined?

First, Congress must have the political will, rectitude and the numbers to effectively countermand EO's. That said, as it plays out now if Congress disapproves an EO, it can withhold funds. But, to do so requires enactment of a law which must pass muster both in the House and the Senate. The rub: if the law intended to countermand an EO is vetoed by the President, to override that veto requires a 2/3 vote, a super majority, in both chambers of Congress, clearly a politically daunting task indeed. And, of course, there is the laborious process of impeachment and removal of the offending President to remedy the executive overreach. But, again, removal would require a 2/3 majority in the Senate, also a very unlikely outcome.

The alternative means of voiding an EO is if a suit is brought against the President before the Supreme Court and the court invalidates the EO, again a highly unlikely scenario. And, as we all know, the Supreme Court, which has proven to be far less than faithful to the meaning and intent of the Constitution, is often on the wrong side of constitutional questions. Seemingly guided by Chief Justice Hughes's arrogant and insidious assertion in 1941 that "we are under a Constitution, but the Constitution is what the judges say it is", the court's unelected judicial oligarchs--and, yes, judicial legislators--have, over the years, proven to be unreliable defenders of the Constitution.

It should be remembered that Roger Sherman, a principal among the framers, held that the president should not have legislative authority; that his job was to execute the laws and nothing more: "The Executive Branch is nothing more than an institution for carrying the will of the legislature into effect".

Similarly, another principal framer, James Wilson, asserted that "the only powers strictly executive were those of executing laws, appointing officers, not appertaining to, and appointed by, the legislature."

And upon the advice of fellow framer Charles Pinckney, none other than James Madison asserted that the president should have "power to carry into effect the national laws, to appoint to offices in cases not otherwise provided for, and to execute such other powers—not legislative or judiciary--in nature."

In effect, the framers insisted that the Chief Executive could not propose or make legislation under any guise, but, with respect to legislation, was absolutely restricted to executing those laws passed by Congress. Crystal clear, but grossly ignored by today's power elite.

With the tacit consent of a habitually unfaithful Supreme Court, a corrupted Congress, and a complacent citizenry, is it any wonder we've strayed so far from the Constitution?

So, in the absence of a President who might happen to be personally inclined to faithfully adhere to the Constitution, we have little defense against a tyrannical Chief Executive. Thus, if the Supreme Court and Congress are unwilling to restore constitutional order by affirmatively re-establishing the doctrine of separation of powers at the federal level, then, ultimately, and in accordance with the 10th Amendment, it falls to the States and/or the People to take appropriate action to remedy the breach. As James Madison asserted, "...the people have an indubitable, unalienable, and indefeasible right to reform or change their government whenever it be found adverse or inadequate to the purpose of its institution."

In closing, our now tattered and barely recognizable republic which was originally held securely in place by a carefully crafted system of checks and balances and separation of powers is no more. To believe otherwise is wishful thinking, or, worse, delusional.

Since TR, with his 1006 unchallenged EO's, Woodrow Wilson's 3,723 EO's and Obama's in excess of 130 frighteningly EO's, the imperial presidency has clearly taken on a life of its own, unchecked and tyrannical, effectively blurring any similarity to genuine republicanism. In truth, all that holds this sham of a republic in place is the President's *appearance* of faithfulness to the constitution or that the President, whoever he or she might be, will graciously opt not to overstep his or her constitutional authority. But, if history is any authoritative guide, such self-inflicted delusion and misplaced confidence on the part of the electorate can only lead to national disaster.

Going forward, patriots everywhere had best pull out all stops to usher in a Constitution-first conservative takeover in DC. But, that's only half the battle. Once elected, we must hold their corruptible feet to the fire to ensure a full restoration of constitutional order, failing which only the dissolution of these united States by whatever means, violent or peaceful, is most certainly inevitable.

To be clear, EO's aren't a Progressive or Republican problem. EO's are an equal opportunity contagion. Both parties, all modern presidents, Congress, the Supreme Court, and, yes, We the People are culpable. If we deserve and expect better, we will beget better.

Does 2nd Amendment Protect an Individual Right to Bear Arms?

Intuitively, I had always believed that the 2nd Amendment protected my *inherent* right to keep and bear arms for my own personal safety; that this right was derived from "natural law" irrespective of any right to same which may have been specifically granted or denied by either the United States or any of the States.

Further, I had always believed that since the federal government was not specifically granted the right to restrict my right to self-protection, that, in accordance with the enumerated powers of Article 1, Section 8 of the Constitution, the federal government did not have the right to in any way deny my right to self- protection; that, similarly, since the right to self-defense is an inherently natural right that no State could abridge or otherwise deny that right as well.

In light of the recent *District of Columbia v Heller* (2008) decision in which SCOTUS struck down DC's handgun ban as well as its ban on loaded, operable firearms for DC residents' self-defense and the *McDonald v City of Chicago* case which protected the right to keep and bear arms from infringement by local governments, my curiosity got the best of me and I decided to explore the meaning of the 2nd Amendment for myself.

Briefly, this is what the *Heller* decision said: "The Second Amendment protects an individual right to possess a firearm <u>unconnected with service in a militia</u>, and use that arm for <u>traditionally</u> lawful purposes, such as self-defense within the home" and "that the District's ban on handgun possession in the home violates the Second Amendment, as does its prohibition against rendering any lawful firearm in the home operable for the purpose of immediate self-defense." However, SCOTUS tempered its decision by allowing for "prohibitions against possession of weapons by felons or the mentally ill" or "carrying of firearms in sensitive places such as schools and government buildings". In short, the Court ruled that the Amendment's prefatory clause, i.e. "a well-regulated militia being necessary to the security of a free state", serves to clarify the operative clause, i.e. "the right of the people to keep and bear arms, shall not be infringed", but does not limit or expand the scope of the operative clause.

The first thing I discovered is that quite apart from the supercilious and intrusive world of social engineers who continually advocate a wholesale ban on privately owned guns without any allusion to constitutional justification, over the years there really has been a serious and honest difference of opinion among respected constitutional scholars as to the precise meaning of the 2nd Amendment, a difference which the *Heller* and *McDonald* decisions seems to have finally resolved for every American. While *Heller* has affirmatively addressed the 2nd Amendment right of citizens to keep and bear arms who reside within federal territories, the *McDonald* ruling extended that right to the local and state levels as well.

But, first, let's very briefly highlight some authoritative, albeit contradictory, case law on this subject before proceeding further:

1. *Barron v Baltimore* (1833): held that the Bill of Rights applies directly to the federal government—not to state governments. In effect, the court ruled that states could infringe on the Bill of Rights since the Bill of Rights was intended to restrain only the federal government— not state governments.

2. *Nunn v State of Georgia* (1846): held that "the right of the people to keep and bear arms shall not be infringed" and that "the right of the whole people, old and young, men, women and boys, and not militia only, to keep and bear arms of every description, and not such merely as are used by the militia, shall not be infringed, curtailed or broken in upon in the smallest degree."

3. *Cockrum v State of Texas* (1859): ruled that "the right of a citizen to bear arms, in lawful defense of himself or state, is absolute. He does not derive it from the state government. It is one of the 'high powers' delegated directly to the citizen, and 'is excepted out of the general powers of government.' A law cannot be passed to infringe upon or impair it, because it is above the law, and independent of the lawmaking power." (Clearly, at some nuanced variance with *Barron v Baltimore*.)

4. 14th Amendment (1868): to address the possible oppression of freed slaves following the civil war and to ensure that former slaves, among other citizens, were able to keep and bear arms for that purpose,

Congress passed this amendment which provides that states may not "abridge the privileges or immunities of citizens of the United States" or "deprive any person of life, liberty, or property, without due process of law." (If you can't get there one way, try another route.)

5. The *Slaughter-House Cases* (1873): held that only those "privileges and immunities" that "owe their existence" to the US Constitution were protected; thus, the Bill of Rights didn't apply to the states because the Bill of Rights protected basic human rights which existed before the ratification of the Constitution.

6. *United States v Cruikshank* (1876): clarified that the right to keep and bear arms existed before the Constitution but that the 2nd Amendment, indeed the 1st Amendment, were not protected from infringement by the states or by private individuals.

7. *Presser v Illinois* (1886) and *Miller v Texas* (1894): held that the 2nd Amendment didn't directly protect against infringement by the states.

8. *People v Zerillo* (Michigan, 1922): Ruled that "the provision in the Constitution granting the right to all persons to bear arms is a limitation upon the power of the Legislature to enact any law to the contrary. The exercise of a right guaranteed by the Constitution cannot be made subject to the will of the sheriff."

9. *Gitlow v New York* (1925): ruled that the 14th Amendment prohibited states from violating some of the rights of citizens without "due process" but stopped short of "incorporating" all of the Bill of Rights at once.

10. Since *Gitlow*, and only on a case by case basis, courts have held that on the strength of the 14th Amendment's "Due Process Clause", the Bill of Rights is protected against state infringement as well as federal. In effect, the Bill of Rights was "incorporated" into the Due Process Clause vide the generally accepted Theory of Substantive Due Process. (Note: today, the 2nd Amendment is one of the last rights in the Bill of Rights to be incorporated.)

11. *District of Columbia v Heller* (2008): the court ruled that the *Cruikshank* decision failed to properly weigh 14th Amendment protections and that "the inherent right of self-defense has been central to the Second Amendment right."

So, though most states protect the individual right to keep and bear arms, the *McDonald v City of Chicago* ensured that the full force of the 2nd Amendment extended to all localities as well. Particularly in those states where there are no state constitutional safeguards, plaintiffs are especially concerned. Without 2nd Amendment rights to keep and bear arms, gun owners are at the mercy of state legislators, social engineering lobbyists and the like. (Conversely, permitting the feds to interpret our 2nd Amendment rights is equally problematic. What the feds grant can also be denied.)

But, what's behind the *McDonald challenge*? In short, the Illinois state constitution states that "Subject only to the police power, the right of the individual citizen to keep and bear arms shall not be infringed." By failing to "incorporate" 14th Amendment inquiry as was required by *Heller*, in June 2009 the 7th Court of Appeals reaffirmed Illinois' power to ban handguns by relying solely—and erroneously—on the *Cruikshank* decision of 1876, thereby ignoring nearly all other pertinent case law as well.

By contrast, earlier, in April 2009, a three-judge panel of the 9th Circuit (*Nordyke v King*) in California concluded that since "the Right to Keep and Bear Arms is deeply rooted in this Nation's history and tradition," that this right is, therefore, "incorporated" into the 14th Amendment Due Process Clause and applies to the states." This decision was on hold awaiting a SCOTUS decision on the *McDonald v City of Chicago* case. Thus, we had two appellate courts and two divergent views in the same year. The earlier decision relied upon the 14th Amendment as required by *Heller* and the panel opinion relied upon *Cruikshank* which had been overruled by Heller. (How mortal and fallible jurists be?)

So, owing to the contradictory case law subsequent to the US Constitution's adoption in 1787, I opted to simplify my inquiry by examining what our framers had to say about all this. Being the real experts, their correspondence and debates carry considerably more weight for me than do more post-ratification interpretations from either the left or the right.

First, the 2nd Amendment states that *"A well-regulated militia, being necessary to the security of a free state, the right of the people to keep and bear arms, shall not be infringed."*

Like all things constitutional, context is absolutely everything, and both logic and a studious level of caution dictate that the expressed intent of the framers should always take precedence over what might be faulty subsequent interpretation. And rather than weighing and examining a dizzying array of contradictory interpretations, I have found solace by relying upon an "originalist" approach to better capture the meaning of the framers in this regard. It just seems eminently more sensible and the least painful path to follow, an approach we should all keep in mind.

Bearing in mind Thomas Jefferson's admonishment that *"on every question of construction let us carry ourselves back to the time when the Constitution was adopted, recollect the spirit manifested in the debates, and instead of trying what meaning may be squeezed out of the text, or invented against it, conform to the probable one in which it was passed"*, any conclusions as to the framers' intent and, thus, the meaning of the 2nd Amendment, will be left to the objectivity and integrity of the reader.

From what I have read, the intended purpose of the 2nd Amendment was to guarantee the right of the people to keep and bear arms as a check on the standing army and any foreign armies. To wit, Noah Webster and Tench Coxe, the latter an ally and correspondent of James Madison, admonished that "before a standing army can rule, the people must be disarmed; as they are in almost every kingdom in Europe." Similarly, George Mason warned that "the colonies' recent experience with Britain", in which King George's goal had been "to disarm the people...was the best way to enslave them."

Further, it appears that the overarching purpose of the Bill of Rights, the first ten amendments of the Constitution, was to better ensure individual rights by specifically proscribing federal violations of those rights. Thus, in short, "well-regulated militia" did not at all mean Congressional regulation of that militia or, by extension, the regulation of the people's right to keep and bear arms. Also, the text of the Amendment expressly confirms that the right to keep and bear arms is retained "by the people", and not the states. Important to note too is that whenever the word "regulate" appears within the Constitution's text, the Constitution specifies who is to do the regulating and what is being regulated. However, in the 2ⁿᵈ Amendment the term "well regulated" describes a militia--not an army reserve or national guard--but does not define who or what regulates it. Thus, <u>from what I could understand, the framers intended that the people comprise an essentially unorganized militia which may, of necessity, be organized and well-regulated, but by the people themselves</u>.

This view is confirmed by Alexander Hamilton (Federalist, No. 29): "... but if circumstances should at any time oblige the government to form an army of any magnitude, that army can never be formidable to the liberties of the people, while there is a large body of citizens, little if at all inferior to them in discipline and use of arms, who stand ready to defend their rights..." Thus, it also appears to have been clearly intended by the framers that law-abiding armed citizens could collectively organize and train and that doing so would not necessarily pose a threat to their fellow citizens, but would, in fact, help "to ensure domestic tranquility" and "provide for the common defence".

But, rather than further wading through a plethora of interesting, albeit esoteric, and often contradictory opinions let's take a brief look at some notable quotes of the framers themselves to better understand their meaning and intent with respect to the 2ⁿᵈ Amendment. It's just more edifying—for me anyway:

1. "No freeman shall ever be debarred the use of arms..." Thomas Jefferson

2. "The people have the right to bear arms for the defense of themselves and the state..." Pennsylvania Declaration of 1776

3. "Americans have the right and advantage of being armed—unlike citizens of other countries whose governments are afraid to trust people with arms." James Madison, Federalist Paper #46

4. "Arms in the hands of individual citizens may be used at individual discretion...in private self-defense." John Adams, 1787

5. "The right of the people to keep and bear arms shall not be infringed. A well- regulated militia, composed of the body of the people, trained

to arms, is the best and most natural defense of a free country..."
James Madison, 1789

6. "...the ultimate authority...resides in the people alone." James Madison

7. "Congress have no power to disarm the militia. <u>Their swords, and every other terrible implement of the soldier, are the birthright of an American</u>. The unlimited power of the sword is not in the hands of either the federal or state government, but, where I trust in God it will ever remain, in the hands of the people." Tench Coxe, 1788

8. "The militia, when properly formed, are in fact the people themselves...and include all men capable of bearing arms." Richard Henry Lee, 1788

9. "The Constitution shall never be construed...to prevent the people of the United States who are peaceable citizens from keeping and bearing arms." Samuel Adams, 1788

10. "To preserve liberty, it is essential that the whole body of people always possess arms, and be taught alike especially when young, how to use them." Richard Henry Lee, 1788

11. "The best we can hope for concerning the people at large is that they be properly armed." Alexander Hamilton

12. "And what country can preserve its liberties, if its rulers are not warned from time to time that this people preserve the spirit of resistance?" Thomas Jefferson

13. "The strongest reason for people to retain the right to keep and bear arms is, as a last resort, to protect themselves against tyranny in government." Thomas Jefferson

14. "Firearms stand next in importance to the Constitution itself. They are the American people's liberty teeth and keystone under independence...To ensure peace, security and happiness, the rifle and pistol are equally indispensable...The very atmosphere of firearms

everywhere restrains evil interference…When firearms go, all goes. We need them every hour." George Washington

While there are also many luminaries, like Einstein, Machiavelli, Ayn Rand, Blackstone, et. al, who celebrate the individual right to keep and bear arms, there are notable detractors as well:

1. "Gun registration is not enough; the most effective way of fighting crime in the United States is to outlaw the possession of any type of firearm by the civilian population." Janet Reno. Atty General, 1991

2. "Our task of creating a socialist America can only succeed when those who would resist us have been totally disarmed." Sara Brady, Chairman, Handgun Control, 1994

3. **"…Our ultimate goal—total control of all guns—is going to take time. The first problem is to slow down the increasing number of handguns being produced and sold in this country. The second problem is to get handguns registered, and the final problem is to make possession of all handguns, and all handgun ammunition totally illegal."** Nelson Shields, Handgun Control

4. "What good does it do to ban some guns. All guns should be banned." Sen. Howard Metzanbaum, 1994

5. "Citizens! Turn in your weapons." (English translation of Soviet Union poster 1919.)

FYI: Current US Code defines militia like this: "The militia of the United States consists of all able-bodied males at least 17 years of age. The classes of the militia are (1) the organized militia, which consists of the National Guard, and (2) *the unorganized militia, which consists of the members in the militia who are not members of the National Guard.*" Title 10, Section 311(a) of the United States Code.

And, finally, no discussion of the 2nd Amendment can be properly wrapped up without this incisive quote from Thomas Jefferson's "Commonplace Book": *False is the idea of utility that sacrifices a thousand real advantages for one imaginary of trifling inconvenience; that would take fire from men because it burns, and water because one may drown in it; that has no remedy for evil, except destruction. The laws that forbid the carrying of arms are laws of such nature…Such laws make things worse for the assaulted and better for the assailants; they serve rather to encourage than prevent homicides, for an unarmed man may be attacked with greater confidence than an armed man…"* --Cesare Beccaria, *On Crimes and Punishments* 87-88 *(H. Paulucci transl. 1963).-- (Thomas Jefferson copied this passage in full in his* Commonplace Book 314 *which was "the source book and repertory of Jefferson's ideas on government." Id. at 4.)*

So, there you have it. Shouldn't the Framers' understanding of the 2nd Amendment be rendered more authoritative than the stream of conspicuously contradictory legal opinions regurgitated over the years? The age-old controversy. As said, for me the Framers' clearly stated opinions as to their meaning and intent necessarily hold sway.

POSTSCRIPT:

Currently under intense assault by Progressives at both the federal and state levels, the inviolability of the 2nd Amendment hangs in the balance. Push-back is widespread, and already there are hundreds of Sheriffs who, within their jurisdictions, have refused to obey these unconstitutional infringements on the right of the people to keep and bear arms. Many States have taken action to nullify federal gun control laws. Stay tuned. This could get very messy.

US Census & the Constitution

For the purpose of apportioning Congressional representation, Article 1, Section 2 of the Constitution states that an "Enumeration shall be made within three Years after the first meeting of the Congress of the United States, and within every subsequent Term of ten Years, <u>in such Manner as they shall by Law direct.</u>" (Clearly, the last eight words are subject to interpretation.)

By definition, a census is "the periodic official count of the number of persons and their condition and of the resources of a country." Located within the Dept. of Interior in 1902, in 1903 it was transferred to the Commerce & Labor Dept. and, for all practical purposes, is currently supervised by the White House.

Omitting Indians not taxed, the first census was conducted under the aegis of the State Department in August of 1790 and elicited the name & number of heads of households, the age & number of white males, the number of white females, the number of all other free persons, and the number of slaves who were counted, for purposes of apportionment, as three-fifths of a person. (Note: the 3/5 stipulation was subsequently removed by the 14th Amendment and the Attorney General ruled in 1940 that there were no longer any "untaxed" Indians in the USA.) Failure to cooperate with the census taker was punishable by a $20 fine. Failure of a census taker to properly record information or to submit a false return was punishable by a $200 - $800 fine.

Now conducted by law (13 USC 141) o/a April 1st every ten years, the Census elicits a relatively straightforward and unintrusive enumeration of persons residing within a particular residence: name, gender, age, race.

On the other hand, the mandatory and considerably more comprehensive <u>American Community Survey (ACS)</u> questionnaire, which is distributed to a randomly chosen 3,000,000 households, elicits not only the number of persons, but such things as the size of the house, personal disabilities, rental and insurance costs, property taxes, utility expenses, sexual orientation, religion, marital status, divorce status, education level, whether you own a vehicle or receive food stamps, occupants' income, health insurance coverage, languages spoken, employment status, etc., etc.

Per Title 13, Section 221 of the US Code, refusal to answer any of the 11-page 48-question ACS exposes respondents to a fine equivalent to $100 per unanswered question and $500 per question answered untruthfully, up to an aggregate of $5,000.

It is important to note, however, that since Article 1, Sec 2, Clause 3 of the Constitution authorizes enumeration only, many constitutional experts opine that while the mechanical manner in which the enumeration is conducted is within the purview of Congress, asking a superfluity of questions beyond simple enumeration may be unconstitutional.

Importantly, the constitutionality of Title 13, Sec 221 itself has never been specifically challenged in court. As such, I suspect this is why the Census Bureau has, heretofore, not imposed any fines. However, the Census Bureau can be expected to dog noncompliant respondents in order to obtain a completed ACS questionnaire.

In any event, case law suggests lingering legal concerns.

In *US v Moriarity (SDNY 1901)*, the district court ruled that the Constitution provides Congress the authority to collect "statistics" in the census "if necessary and proper" for the efficient exercise of other federal powers enumerated in the Constitution.

As early as 1870, the Supreme Court rendered unquestionable the authority of Congress to require both enumeration and collection of statistics.

In *Morales v Daley (TX, 2000)*, another District Court ruled that there was "no limit" on the collection of additional data when necessary for efficient governance, adding that eliciting additional information did not violate a citizen's right to privacy and speech.

Also, in *Dept. of Commerce v House of Representatives (1999)*, the Supreme Court described the census as "the linchpin of the federal system... collecting data on characteristics on individuals, households, and housing units throughout the country", thus underscoring the importance of enumeration and the collection of additional statistics.

Obviously, the substance of those additional questions and statistics which may, in fact, be "necessary and proper" for efficient and constitutional governance remains essentially undefined. And that is the nub of the issue for me.

Thus, among others, Dr. Walter Williams, George Mason University, and Congresswoman Michele Bachman asserted they would provide only the number and names of the people in their household during the 2010 census. Nothing more. If pressed by census takers, Dr. Williams counseled that respondents should exercise their 5th Amendment right to remain silent.

In reaction to the anger and trepidation of many Americans over what may be fairly construed as invasive ACS questioning, Rep. Ted Poe (R-TX) recently introduced HR 3131 which would make participation in the ACS strictly voluntary--except for the respondent's name, contact info, date of response, and no. of person living or staying at the residence.

For me, concerns over the constitutionality of the ACS and the confidentiality of respondents' answers are of no small concern. Thus, what course of action respondents take when asked to respond to an ACS questionnaire is really a matter of conscience and choice. As said, the constitutionality of the ACS is certainly unsettled.

POSTSCRIPT: HR 3131 died in Committee

Term Limits Needed to Restore Trust & Integrity

I think we can agree that D.C. is broken, and that a restoration of limited, civic-minded and responsive governance is long overdue. The question is how do we bring that about. From my preliminary research, I have concluded that term limits is at the core of any meaningful remedy.

Though polls suggest that nearly 80% of the people support term limits, in *US Term Limits v Thornton*, 514 US 779 (1995) the Supreme Court narrowly ruled 5-4 that state-imposed term limits on members of Congress was unconstitutional and that only if the Constitution is amended may term limits be imposed.

Citing that since authority to limit congressional term limits was not specifically reserved to the States, Justice Stevens reflected the majority opinion by stating that "in the absence of any constitutional delegation to the States of power to add qualifications to those enumerated in the Constitution, such a [State] power does not exist." (A rather contrived, twisted view of the 10th Amendment, I'd say.)

Further, *Storer vs Brown* granted States the right to regulate election procedures but not to impose qualifications for Senators and Representatives. (It is important to note, however, that Justice Thomas dissented by opining that "where the Constitution does not speak either expressly or by necessary implication, the Federal Government lacks that power and the States enjoy it." Makes sense to me.)

From my preliminary research of this subject, by the very fact that the Framers carefully omitted senatorial and representative qualifications for office—except age, citizenship and residency—it seems reasonable to conclude that the founding fathers may have left the issue of term limits to the People alone and not to the States or to the federal government--either that, or the omission of term limits was an oversight. This conclusion would be consistent with Dr. Robert Livingston's view that "the people are the best judge of who ought to represent them." However, it has become apparent to me that the Framers' views on this subject were sometimes ambiguous and their positions on the matter often imprecise.

However, it's important to note that Thomas Jefferson believed that the Framers' failure to include term limits in the Constitution was one of two "principal flaws"--the other being the absence of a bill of rights (Ltr from Jefferson to Madison, 12/20/1787). Thus, his respect for the notion of term limits is obvious.

Interestingly, James Madison noted that term limits may be one of the "effectual precautions" which will better ensure that the people keep their representatives "virtuous whilst they continue to hold their public trust". (Federalist Paper #57). In Federalist Paper #39, he conceded that "tenure for a limited period" was a defining characteristic of representatives in a republican form of government.

George Mason, another Framer, considered "periodical rotation essential to the preservation of republican government."

So, though there appears to be plenty of Framer support for the concept of term limits, the Framers clearly saw no need to set term limits in the Constitution itself since they assumed frequent elections would result in regular turnover in both houses anyway. To wit, James Madison anticipated that "new members would always form a large proportion" of the House.

Some Framers actually anticipated a 2/3 turnover in congressional membership. Obviously, they did not foresee that their assumptions regarding a high turnover of members would be so at odds with actual developments in modern day America. They never guessed that about 90% of today's well-financed incumbents would be virtually assured of re-election and that civic-minded "citizen representatives" committed to temporary public service would be the exception, not the rule.

There are numerous arguments for and against term limits, but the following constitutes the nub of the issue for me: many argue that representatives need more time to learn the ropes, thus enhancing their effectiveness as lawmakers; however, this assertion refutes itself. Simply put, we limit the President to two 4-year terms. Is the President's job so much less demanding and complex that we can limit his tenure to 8 years, but a Senator or Representative needs more time?

Also, the biggest and most cogent argument against State-imposed term limits is this: Justice Stevens opined that "permitting individual states to formulate diverse qualifications for their congressional representatives would result in a patchwork that would be inconsistent with the Framers' vision of a *uniform* national legislature representing the people of the US." Hard to logically counter that argument. It could, indeed, be a mess. Thus, it would seem that only a constitutional amendment can achieve the desired uniformity.

Also, what appears disturbingly obvious to me is that for a long time now unresponsive and seemingly disconnected--even clueless--political careerists have often controlled the reins of legislative power. Obviously, that is not what the Framers had in mind for our republic. Thus, for me, term limits is the only remedy to cronyism and self-serving careerism.

Among other benefits, term limits will: 1) encourage new folks with fresh ideas, 2) encourage representatives to fashion policy on the basis of principles vs. the demands of re-election campaigns, 3) limit the level of corruption and the inordinate and counterproductive influence of lobbyists, 4) prevent the growth and entrenchment of a permanent ruling class more interested in feathering its own nest than in properly representing the legitimate interests of electoral constituencies and their country, and 5) term limits might well moderate the damaging effects of gerrymandering.

Watching aged reps barely able to walk or coherently speak suggests to me that to better ensure accountability and to restore congressional relevance and competence, perhaps the most sensible term limit solution lies somewhere in the commonsense middle.

I opt for no more than three consecutive 2-year terms for Representatives (total 6 yrs) and no more than two consecutive 6-year terms for Senators (total 12 yrs). And to ensure that the people, the ultimate guardians of our republican form of government, are able to determine who should represent them in D.C., at the conclusion of their term limit a Senator or Representative would be permitted to run for a seat in the other chamber, thus ensuring that the electorate is not denied the future services of an especially popular favorite son whose tenure in one chamber has expired.

Also, to retain the people's authority over who will represent them in D.C., a tenured-out Senator or Representative may opt to seek re-election in the same chamber, but only after a requisite two (House) or six (Senate) year break in his or her service in that chamber. This formula would also ensure that a lame duck rep who is still interested in public office at a later date would strive to be productive, responsive, energetic and engaged until the conclusion of his tenure. Representatives' talents wouldn't be wasted, "institutional memory" wouldn't be lost, a more vigorous competition of ideas would ensue, a "citizen congress" vs a mob of lobby-dominated career politicians would blossom once again, and otherwise entrenched congressional staffers with, perhaps, questionable lobbyist ties themselves would be replaced more frequently with fresh blood. Upshot: "we the people" would, at long last, be better served. At least that's my take.

Though the amendment process normally takes years, I'm convinced that we need to move the process forward. So, let's light the fire under both our DC and State representatives to begin the amendment process, whether that process originates with Congress or the States.

As we all know too well, of course, a ruling bureaucracy is never self-correcting, and an entrenched elite even less so; thus, it will clearly require an intensely hot flame to move things forward.

[4] IMPEACHMENT

If Not Impeachment, What? (1/2011)

Sobered and deeply troubled by Progressives' determination to completely undermine what precious little remains of this Republic, it becomes crystal-clear that a genial solution to our nation's challenges is likely impossible.

So, what can we do? Well, I think we can eliminate impeachment as a realistic remedy.

Bear in mind that impeachment (indictment) is a ***political***--not a legal--process. A majority in the House of Representatives can impeach, but <u>2/3 of the Senate</u> (trial) is required to convict and remove a sitting President. And because it is such an onerous and highly politicized process, only two Chief Executives, Andrew Johnson and William Clinton, have ever been impeached, though, significantly, neither of them was convicted and removed from office.

Given the extensive Progressive contagion which has swept DC, both on the left and the right, the chances of successfully applying this two-step process is, therefore, very, very remote. As things now stand, it appears only a flagrant act of presidential treason or murder would persuade the House and Senate to respectively impeach and remove a Chief Executive— much less a faithless Supreme Court justice.

Briefly, despite deliberate and all too often successful political attempts over the years to misinterpret the meaning of "high crimes and misdemeanors", my research manifestly renders Obama both impeachable and removable. Why? We must remember that "high crimes and misdemeanors" aren't restricted to murder and treason. In fact, our Founders considered maladministration, *breach of public trust, abuse of power, negligence and, yes, even immoral behavior, among others*, as impeachable offenses.

In essence, **an impeachable offense is not necessarily an indictable offense and an indictable offense is not necessarily an impeachable offense**. Simply put, an impeachable offense is WHATEVER Congress may say it is at any given time.

That said, I refer you to Canada Free Press which has creditably kept track of Obama's impeachable offenses--50+, so far. As of today, we may be able to add several others, among those being Benghazigate (selling arms to Islamists) and committing US military assets to Libya without Congressional approval. Thus, while the CFP list is hardly exhaustive, it fairly highlights some of the more egregious offenses so far committed by this imperial president. In their totality, these offenses are breathtaking in scope and seriousness. But, again, ONLY if the House indicts, and ONLY if the Senate convicts can this smug imperial ideologue be removed.

From my lowly vantage point, Obama is, hands-down, the most impeachable chief executive in our nation's history. And because he is constitutionally ineligible for re-election in 2016--this despite an odious proposal by Congressman Jose Serrano (D-NY 15th), member of the ***Democratic Socialists of America***, to eliminate presidential term limits--short of impeachment, conviction or incapacity we have only our God-given natural and constitutional rights of resistance, e.g. civil disobedience, State nullification, secession and rebellion, to shield us from Obama's brazen utopian transformation of this union and to prevent our slide into economic oblivion. And to rely on the federal courts to support the Constitution against this Progressive thug is extremely doubtful.

So, yes, folks, sorry to say, but the remedy is now squarely on our shoulders and on the shoulders of our respective States to resist. We can rely on nothing else. Wishful thinking, benign neglect, and prayers alone won't turn the tide and save this country. And with both our 1st and 2nd

Amendment rights under attack, now more than ever patriots need to be solidly united. Are we up to it? That remains to be seen...

("Our unalienable rights are unalienable only to the extent that we are willing to defend them." Jim Delaney)

Obama: Is Impeachment a Viable Option? (8/2011)

On the internet, there has been considerable talk about impeaching Obama. Though surely an attractive solution to the "Obama Problem", impeachment simply isn't as easily accomplished as many of us would like to believe it is.

And when the likes of former Rep. Dennis Kucinich (D-OH) condemns Obama for his UN-sanctioned Libyan military intervention without having secured Congressional approval beforehand, one is apt to believe that impeachment might well be that much closer to reality. Well, that's simply not so. Have you noticed how congressional talk of impeachment has all but disappeared?

Over the past several years in particular, an increasingly imperious executive has rapidly transformed the Office of the President into something only remotely resembling the executive office described in Art II of the Constitution. Though this transformation has been developing for some time now--aided and abetted by Congress, of course--the unseemly growth in presidential power appears to have been on an especially steep ascent since Obama's inauguration in 2009.

Short of Congress's faithfully and resolutely restoring the separation of powers between the Executive and Legislative branches, what is the constitutional solution to what many might describe as Obama's misconduct? Impeachment? Well, let's take a look.

Article II, Sec 4 of the Constitution states that "The President, Vice President and all civil officers of the United States, shall be removed from Office on Impeachment for, and Conviction of, **Treason, Bribery, or other high Crimes and Misdemeanors**."

First off, **it is important to understand that impeachment is NOT a legal process. It is a political process;** thus, though the Founders' words "high crimes and misdemeanors" were intentionally broad to encompass nearly ANY misconduct or misbehavior while in office, in the final analysis impeachment remains a political matter. In short, where there is congressional will and consensus, there will be impeachment.

As Pres. Ford so aptly asserted when asked what an impeachable offense was, he replied that **"an impeachable offense is whatever a majority of the House of Representatives considers it to be at a given moment in history."** And, of course, impeachment is only part of the story. Conviction and removal from office still requires the approval of 2/3 of the Senate. No small feat, especially if the Senate is dominated by a party politically sympathetic to the President.

That said, to better clarify the meaning of Art II, Sec 4, let's briefly examine some definitions as well as what the Constitution's framers and ratifiers understood those words to have meant.

Based on English common law, "impeach" means to *indict* a person for misconduct while in office, and in the case of the United States indictment for purposes of impeachment falls solely within the purview of the House of Representatives.

Drawing on England's Treason Act of 1351, the framers limited **treason** to "levying War (declared or undeclared) against [the United States], or in adhering to their Enemies, giving them Aid and Comfort." The word "comfort" meant "support" or "assistance". As required in Article III Sec 3 for a person to be convicted of treason, two witnesses to the act or a confession in open court was needed.

Again based on English law, it is important to note that "high crimes and misdemeanors" is not synonymous with an indictable "crime" or "misdemeanor". Also, "high" connotes misbehavior or a breach of fiduciary duty, aka breach of public trust, while in office.

In his Commentaries on the Laws of England (1757), which was a primary reference for American legal scholars in the 18th century, Sir Wm Blackstone asserted that "the first and principal [high misdemeanor] is the maladministration of such high officers, as are in the public trust and employments. This is usually punished by the method of parliamentary impeachment." In other words, while mal-administration may not be in and of itself an indictable crime mal-administration can be an impeachable offense. Blackstone further elaborated on the meaning of "neglect", or *misprision*, by pointing out that "THE principal *misprision* is the mal-administration of such high officers, as are in public trust and employments".

Wm. Petty's <u>Jus Parliamentarium</u> (1740) enumerated examples of conduct justifying impeachment on the grounds of breaches in public trust, those being self-dealing, neglect, misdirection of funds, and the misuse of the pardon powers.

John Comyn's <u>Digest of the Laws of England</u> (1780) also defined "high crimes and misdemeanors" as violations of public trust, among those being violations of criminal law, acting outside authority, issuing unlawful and irregular orders, self-dealing, other disloyal conduct such as recommending a prejudicial peace, and negligence.

In the <u>Institutes</u> (1765) by Edward Coke, another primary legal source of our framers, examples of breaches of fiduciary trust were variously described as self-dealing, neglect of duty, misdirection of funds, and, interestingly, misuse of pardon power. Among other breaches included violations of criminal law, such as encouraging piracy and bribery, acting outside authority, as by ratifying a peace not approved by the parties, using the Great Seal w/o permission, issuing unlawful and irregular orders, attempting to undermine religion, delaying court proceedings, refusing to carry out one's duties, and violating one's fiduciary duty.

Among our Founders, James Madison argued that "an impeachment procedure for the President was necessary because it was indispensable that some provision should be made for defending the Community against the incapacity, negligence or perfidy of the chief Magistrate...He might lose his capacity after his appointment. He might pervert his administration into a scheme of peculation or oppression. He might betray his trust to foreign powers."

George Mason believed impeachment was appropriate in instances of "corruption", and Charles Pinkney believed it should be relied upon when public officers "**behave amiss** or betray their public trust."

William Rawles, an early 19th century constitutional scholar, considered "the inordinate extension of power, the influence of party and of prejudice" and attempts to "infringe the rights of the people" as grounds for impeachment.

Also, Alexander Hamilton, though a fervent proponent of a strong Executive, observed that "from the very circumstance of his being alone, the President will be more narrowly watched and more readily suspected." He believed impeachment should be relied upon in cases of "negligence and perfidy", the latter meaning faithlessness or treachery. Thus, <u>the standard of conduct for the President was intended to be much higher than for officers in the legislative or judicial branches of government.</u>

Since 1789, Congress has initiated 64 impeachment proceedings, the most recent being against Judge Porteous, US District Court for the Eastern District of Louisiana, who was convicted in 2010. Also, as a federal judge, Rep. Alcee Hastings (D-FL) was impeached and convicted for bribery in 1989, but since Congress did not prohibit his holding public office despite conviction, he currently serves in Congress as a representative of Florida. (Clearly, our representatives really do reflect our values or lack thereof.)

Among the Presidents, Wm Clinton and Andrew Johnson were impeached but not convicted. (Nixon resigned before the articles of impeachment drawn up in the House against him could be acted upon by House members.)

As Robert Natelson summarized in <u>The Original Constitution</u>, "the Constitution's grounds for impeachment may be summarized as (1) treason, (2) bribery, or (3) other breaches of public trust—such as serious violations of law, disloyalty, self-dealing, abuse of power, failing to account for funds, and negligence in performance of duty. *That negligence was a ground for impeachment demonstrates that an official might be removed for failure to act properly as well as for **acting wrongfully**.*"

In <u>The Lessons of Impeachment History</u> (1999), Prof. M. Gerhardt, College of Wm. & Mary Law School, presented a cogent and careful examination of impeachment, and it is well worth reading. In his exposition, he noted that <u>"the founders did not regard political crimes to be the functional equivalent of indictable crimes nor all indictable crimes to constitute impeachable offenses."</u> He explained that impeachable offenses require **"a serious injury to the political order or to the**

constitutional system" and **"involve the serious misuse of office or official prerogatives or breaches of the public trusts held."** Thus, as a practical matter, the legitimacy of an impeachment procedure is contingent upon public opinion and, by extension therefore, Congress's disposition. Thus, it more clearly appears that Pres. Ford's terse opinion on what constitutes an impeachable offense is not only succinct, but entirely accurate.

As said, the precise meaning of "high crimes and misdemeanors" was never clearly defined by the founders which appeared to have been intentional. During the Constitutional Convention in 1787, the framers described "mal-" and "corrupt administration" as well as "neglect of duty", "malversation" (improper behavior in office), and "misconduct in office" as impeachable offenses.

Notably, framer James Iredell acknowledged how difficult it was to precisely define the scope of impeachable offenses, asserting that such would "involve serious injustices to the federal government"--subjective to be sure and requiring congressional consensus that said offenses were, in fact, impeachable.

Among specific impeachable Presidential offenses delineated by Iredell were 1) providing "false information to the Senate", and 2) "accepting a bribe or acting from a corrupt nature." However, he cautioned against punishing a President for "want of judgment", but considered it appropriate to hold the President accountable for being a "villain" and "willfully abusing his trust".

Interestingly, James Madison suggested that an impeachable offense on the part of the President is if he has **"suspicious connections** with others." Again, this is subjective and requires congressional consensus as to what may, in fact, constitute "suspicious connections".

Regarding the words "high" and "misdemeanor", framer James Wilson defined them as simply "political" and "misconduct" respectively.

Of special importance to me is Prof. Gerhardt's understanding that impeachable acts must be "malicious in nature" and "intended to expand one's powers beyond constitutional limits."

Again, it appears that the founders deliberately left the definition of "high crimes and misdemeanors"-- which connote political crimes to the exclusion of indictable criminal acts--to the sole interpretation and discretion of Congress, the electorate and the judgment of history, the latter which most congresspersons would likely carefully weigh when assessing whether or not an act was impeachable. The framers assumed that no legislator would want to invite the opprobrium of future historians by their recklessness or lack of judiciousness.

Prof. Gerhardt explained that to the founders the **character** of an office holder was also of supreme importance. As he observed, while prevaricating about a non-official activity (as in the Monica Lewinsky affair) may not equate to an office holder's violating public trust, merely the commission of such an act might very well impact how the public and Congress might view an office holder's overall suitability, trust worthiness, "moral authority" and, of course, his impeachability. Thus, for the pundits and Clinton supporters to have suggested that Clinton's lying under oath did not "rise to the level of impeachable offense" was not only inaccurate, it was also deceptive, for in the final analysis only the House can determine whether a President's misconduct is impeachable, and only the Senate can convict and remove a President from office.

Prof. Gerhardt concluded that the founders' views as well as our historical impeachment experience itself suggest that the founders believed that Congress must always strive never to impeach purely for partisan reasons. In short, Congress must always eschew "retaliation" or "punishment" simply as an expression of opposition to the President's "opinions, policy differences, or innocent errors of judgment" He studiously observes that impeachment should be carefully restricted to "misconduct that has caused serious injury to the Republic or to the constitutional system."

With these definitions and the framers' explanations in mind, and fully understanding that congressional consensus is controlling, one should be able to more readily discern what conduct exhibited by our Chief Magistrate at any given time is most likely an impeachable offense. And if we are convinced a particular act is impeachable, it is, in turn, incumbent upon us to influence our congressional representatives to adopt the same view.

Last but not least, the political affiliation of the party in control of Congress is THE determining factor as to whether or not an impeachment or conviction is feasible. And unless a President's actions are especially egregious and offensive to both parties or at least to a majority in the House and 2/3 in the Senate, only the ballot box--or rebellion--can effectively remove him from office.

[5] NULLIFICATION

Nullification Redux:
Resisting Progressive Tyranny (10/2009)

Recently, a friend and I were lamenting the steady dissolution of our Constitution. It seemed to us that the further our politicians have strayed from the meaning and intent of the Constitution, the more enervated, disunited and dispirited our nation and its people have become.

Discussing how best to reverse the decline and to restore Constitutional governance, we briefly alluded to the discredited doctrine of nullification about which neither of us knew very much at all. So, I decided to briefly revisit the subject to see what I could learn. In a nutshell, this is it. I hope it will be of some interest to you.

The Constitution's 10th Amendment unambiguously provides that *"the powers not delegated to the United States by the Constitution, nor prohibited by it to the States, are reserved to the States respectively, or to the people."*

Over the years, the federal government's loose and expansive interpretation of the Constitution has steadily led to federal encroachment on state powers and individual rights at a pace and breadth not clearly foreseen by the Founders, leaving this country and its people more divided and polarized than since immediately prior to the "Civil War".

Awakened to Obama's threat of "fundamentally transforming" America, and much to the consternation of the Progressives currently dominating the national political scene, many states and many grassroots Americans are now vigorously pushing back and asserting their Constitutional rights of sovereignty and individual liberty. We can only hope it's not too late.

Since Obama's election in 2009, Congress has unleashed a transformational legislative blitzkrieg surpassing that of the New Deal which boldly challenges both state sovereignty and individual freedoms as never before. The resulting uneasiness in the country manifestly belies the hollowness of Obama's hope-and-change and no-blue-or-red-states-but-American sloganeering. To wit, with Obama's election and the Progressive entrenchment in DC, not only have gun sales skyrocketed, but, quite unexpectedly, state nullification laws intended to restrain further federal usurpations have ballooned. Clearly, the folks and the States wherein they reside are growing justifiably wary.

Since 1865, nullification was viewed as a moribund curiosity which, while having often impacted our country in the past, had essentially become an eccentricity, a nullity in the post "Civil War" era. But, as I soon discovered, nullification has returned with a vengeance.

In the Fourth Edition of *Black's Law Dictionary*, nullification, aka interposition, is defined as "the doctrine that a state, in the exercise of its sovereignty, may reject a mandate of the federal government deemed to be unconstitutional or to exceed the powers delegated to the federal government. The doctrine denies constitutional obligations of States to respect Supreme Court decisions with which they do not agree." Indeed, the American Revolution, grounded in Magna Carta principles, was a successful act of nullification, secession and forcible resistance. On the other hand, the so-called American "Civil War", aka "War of Northern Aggression", "Lincoln's War", "War of Southern Secession", "War for Southern Independence", was a notable and costly violation of the nullification doctrine.

Essentially, the nullification doctrine is predicated on the theory that sovereign States comprise the union, and as architects of the compact which formed that union, hold final authority regarding the limits of federal power. Conversely, the "national sovereignty", aka "nationalist", theory argues that the Supremacy Clause in Article VI of the Constitution absolutely guarantees federal government supremacy over the States in every way.

However, the "compact" theory persuasively asserts that the Supremacy Clause expressly states that the Constitution *"and all laws made pursuant to it"* are supreme--NOT the federal government or any laws or rulings it may promulgate. Further and very importantly, "compact" adherents argue that federal powers are not inherent, but, as demonstrated by Article 1 Section 8 of the Constitution, were specifically delegated by the States to the federal government as a pre-condition of the Constitution's adoption. In effect, the compact between the States and the federal government provides that the States surrender specific powers to the federal government but that they maintain those powers not specifically delegated. (In Federalists 32 & 33, Alexander Hamilton espoused the compact theory, as did Thomas Jefferson. On the other hand, I discovered that James Madison, though clearly wedded to the compact theory in the Kentucky and Virginia Resolution of 1798, seems to have, over time, become conflicted and often inexplicably contradictory on this point.)

In any event, once again the "compact theory" is being advanced. Intended to publicly challenge federal usurpation of State sovereignty, this year many State legislatures have passed State sovereignty resolutions. These "shots across the bow", so to speak, do not have the force of law, but do serve notice to the federal government to "cease and desist any and all activities" outside the scope of its Article 1, Section 8 delegated powers. In effect, these resolutions put the feds on notice that federal encroachment, aka "acts of usurpation" as expressed in Amendments 9 and 10, will not be routinely submitted to as in the past.

Already this year, Tenth Amendment Resolutions have been passed and signed by the Governors in Alaska and Tennessee, and have passed one or both legislative chambers in Arizona, Georgia, Idaho, Louisiana, Michigan, Mississippi, Missouri, N. Carolina, N. Dakota, Ohio, Oklahoma, S. Carolina, S. Dakota, and Virginia. So, it's not just a southern thing, not by a long shot.

In the following states, at least one legislative chamber has, so far, passed legislation asserting that federal regulation of firearms produced, sold and used within the state is beyond the "commerce clause" authority of Congress: Alaska, Montana, and Tennessee. In several other states, similar legislation has been introduced. (Note: to avoid a needless clash, Montana has also opted to test its sovereignty in this regard by submitting its jurisdictional contention to judicial review.) If one can achieve one's goals peacefully, then why not?

Asserting that the imposition of national health care plans is unconstitutional, Arizona, New Mexico, Wyoming, N. Dakota, Minnesota, Indiana, Michigan, Ohio, W. Virginia, Pennsylvania and Florida have introduced legislation to effectively nullify any such federal plan.

Of special interest too is that while the Montana State House also unanimously condemned the REAL ID Act as an improper use of federal legislative power, what was particularly significant is that the bill condemning the Act stipulated that "the legislature of the state of Montana hereby nullifies the REAL ID Act of 2005, as it would apply in this state," thus underscoring the seriousness of its resistance.

To blunt the takeover of State sovereignty, these particular States are pushing back hard, openly and seriously. The weighty question is whether or not this sudden and widespread state resistance can persuade the feds to back off, or whether this clash over the inviolability of the Constitution's separation of powers doctrine might eventually lead to conflict and/or secession.

So, though some of us may have thought that Appomattox settled the question of nullification and secession, it is now abundantly clear that it did not. In fact, the principle of nullification, aka "interposition", is deeply entrenched in the history of the United States.

In 1793, Georgia successfully nullified the Supreme Court's ruling in *Chisholm v Georgia* that an individual could sue a State in federal court without the State's permission. Most States agreed and the 11th Amendment was soon passed which prohibited such suits. This illustrated the fact that even if both houses of Congress refused to initiate an amendment process that two-thirds of the States could peacefully compel Congress to call a Constitutional Convention to remedy federal breaches of the Constitution.

Some may recall that in 1798 the legislatures of Virginia and Kentucky, in protest of the Alien and Sedition Acts, resolved that if the federal government presumed to possess the sole authority to determine the extent of its powers, that its power would eventually be unbridled and could, therefore, lead to tyranny. In effect, the Virginia and Kentucky Resolution (authored by James Madison and Thomas Jefferson respectively) asserted that States not only possessed the right, but were "duty bound" to nullify unconstitutional federal laws.

As Thomas Jefferson wrote, "When all government, domestic and foreign, in little as in great things, shall be drawn to Washington as the center of all power, it will render powerless the checks provided of one government on another, and will become as venal and oppressive as the government from which we separated."

Hard hit by the Embargo of 1807-1809, and in opposition to the finding in *United States v The William* in 1808 which ruled the embargo constitutional, the Massachusetts assembly effectively overruled the court by asserting that any State could refuse "assistance, aid or cooperation" when any federal act is unconstitutional. The Connecticut assembly went further by directing that all State officials actively withhold "any official aid or co-operation in the execution of the act," the very definition of "anti-commandeering", a less punitive form of nullification. The embargo quickly unraveled.

The Connecticut General Assembly declared: "Resolved, that to preserve the Union, and support the Constitution of the United States, it becomes the duty of the...states, in such a crisis...vigilantly to watch over, and vigorously to maintain, the powers not delegated to the United States, but reserved to the States respectively, or to the people; and that a due regard to this duty, will not permit this Assembly to assist, or concur in giving effect to the aforesaid unconstitutional act, passed, to enforce the embargo." In effect, the Assembly was asserting a State's right to "interpose" their protection between the federal government and the rights and liberties of the people.

In 1812, during America's war with England, the federal government called up the State militias "to execute the Laws of the Union, suppress Insurrections and repel invasions." Massachusetts, and then Connecticut, nullified the call-up on the grounds that "as this power is not [specifically] delegated to the United States by the Constitution, nor prohibited by it to the States, it is reserved to the States, respectively; and from the nature of the power, it must be exercised by those with whom the States have respectively entrusted the chief command of the militia, [that being the Governors of those respective States]." Convinced that the federal government's real ambition was to annex Canada and not merely to defend the union, the Assemblies asserted that unless those States were threatened "by an actual invasion of any portion of [their] territory" that the Commander-in-Chief had no right to call upon the State militias to carry out offensive wars."

In 1813, a more debilitating embargo was imposed. Flooded with grievances, eventually the Massachusetts General Court asserted that "a power to regulate commerce is abused when employed to destroy it." The assertion went on to reject the notion that "the free, sovereign and independent State of Massachusetts [should be] reduced to a mere municipal corporation, without power to protect its people, and to defend them from oppression, from whatever quarter it comes." Again the State affirmed its Constitutional right to "interpose" itself between the oppressor and the people.

Then there was the famous Nullification Crisis of 1832 when S. Carolina undertook to nullify a federal tariff law which led to President Jackson's threatened use of force against a State. Upshot: a compromise tariff was adopted to avert war. Thus, nullification did have the intended effect. (Note: interestingly, though the tariff was oppressive, its imposition was, in fact, constitutional.)

In 1850, several morally enraged northern States resisted federal attempts to enforce the capture and return of runaway slaves. And although the Constitution at the time actually contained a clause to justify enforcement, these States argued that since the Constitution did not specify a clearly defined enforcement mechanism that their compliance would be withheld in those States.

Though there are several other examples of successful nullification initiatives, the point is that the right to nullify and even secede are legitimate constitutional remedies to overweening or intrusive federal authority. And, of course, short of nullification, some states have simply ignored federal mandates, e.g. seatbelt and motorcycle helmet laws,

Daylight Savings Time (AZ and Hawaii), and participation in No Child Left Behind (Utah).

Worth noting too are the following points which I dredged up: Of the original 13 states, Virginia, Rhode Island and Maryland formally conditioned their ratification of the Constitution on the understanding that they explicitly retained the right to secede and the Constitutional Convention never challenged that right. Also, following the so-called "Civil War", and only under duress, the State Constitutions of six of the former Confederate States expressly prohibited their right to secede, though one should bear in mind that there is nothing to prevent those States from formalizing in their Constitutions that which is already an inherent power of the States. Worthy of note too is the fact that the Constitution does not expressly forbid a State from leaving the union. Thus, it would seem that, short of open rebellion, nullification (interposition) and secession still appear to be defensible ways of ensuring that federal excesses--whether executive, congressional or judicial--cannot supersede State sovereignty, the guaranteed rights of the people or the sanctity of the Constitution itself.

The Founders clearly understood and espoused the belief that political leaders are best held accountable to the people when government is local; that decentralization leads to a healthier level of state competition and policy experimentation, thus limiting the scope of damages which can accrue when central planning and experimentation is uniformly imposed throughout the country, the rationale being that it is better that a policy experiment fail in one state than in the entire union.

While some today believe that only the serious threat of secession can effectively roll back the suffocating federal usurpation which has already taken place, those State legislatures named above are hoping that a serious "shot across the bow" will check federal power and avert more serious confrontation. Still others have advanced the idea that the nation has become too large to effectively accommodate the Constitutional plan of governance envisioned by the Founders and that, therefore, the nation needs to peacefully reorganize into smaller administrative units of states, each administrative region acting as an integral part of a confederated republic where the people-to-representative ratio in each region would be more manageable and credible.

Of special concern to many is the increasing power of the Supreme Court to not only re-interpret the Constitution, but to render what many view as unconstitutional and highly polarizing political decisions.

So how do the States and people restrain judicial overreach as well? Robert Hawes in his "Nullification Revisited" explained that while the decisions of Chief Justice John Marshall served to implant the heretofore unshakeable notion that the Supreme Court is and ought to be the final arbiter in all Constitutional matters, **Alexander Hamilton remarked in Federalist 81 that the Constitution does not empower "the national courts to construe the laws according to the *spirit* of the Constitution, or give them any greater latitude in this respect than may be claimed by the courts of every State."** He concluded by stating that "the Constitution ought to be the standard of construction for the laws, and that wherever there is an evident opposition, the laws ought to give place to the Constitution." In effect, Hamilton envisioned the tyranny of a national judicial authority defining its own interpretive powers and "giving it the ability to re-invent itself and evolve beyond its authorized scope." And for me and many other Americans, the courts have, indeed, become dangerously politicized and, therefore, unreliable stewards of the Constitution. Thus, "compact" adherents would suggest that nullification, secession or an Article V Constitutional Convention are the only legal and appropriate means of protecting the Constitution and all the rights which flow from it.

As the Tenth Amendment Center noted in a "talking points" post, "We agree with historian Kevin Gutzman, who has said that those who would give us a 'living Constitution' are actually giving us a dead one, since such a thing is completely unable to protect us against the encroachments of government power." Truer words....

Finally, when torn between protecting one's rights under the Constitution or submissively accommodating federal overreaching and politicized interpretations of the Constitution, what reasonable remedies are left for a state and the people residing therein? Moral suasion, nullification, peaceful secession, violent secession, civil disobedience, convening an Article V Constitutional Convention to redress Constitutional grievances, or simply ignoring unconstitutional federal mandates. For me, whatever works best to preserve the Constitution and to safeguard life, liberty and property is the right solution.

Food for thought in these perilous times.

("Ultimately, whether or not a State is allowed to secede is neither a legal question nor a constitutional question, but rather a matter of political will. How strong is the will of the people in the departing State to be free and independent of the control of the world's only superpower? How far will the US Government be prepared to go in imposing its will on a breakaway republic? Only time will tell." Thomas Naylor, "The Constitutionality of Secession")

("We have given you a Republic, if you can keep it." Benjamin Franklin.*)*

("Each State, in ratifying the Constitution, is considered as a sovereign body, independent of all others, and only to be bound by its own voluntary act. In this relation, then, the new Constitution will, if established, be a federal, and not a national constitution." James Madison, Federalist #39*)*

*Anti-commandeering & Nullification Defined**

Prigg v PA (1842) ruled that States cannot be compelled to use State law enforcement resources to enforce federal law. This "anti-commandeering" doctrine was reaffirmed in *Printz v US* (1997) & *NY v US* (1992) which held that the federal government may not enact a regulatory program that "commandeers" the State's legislative and administrative mechanisms to enforce federal laws. Thus, if a State does not assist in a federal law's enforcement but does not a) declare the federal law unconstitutional and b) does not criminalize its enforcement, then it is "anti-commandeering"- -not nullification. (Example of anti-commandeering is the refusal of 25 States to establish Obamacare health exchanges.) However, refusing to implement an *unconstitutional* act ("unwarrantable") is "nullification" which could include subjecting both State and federal officials to State arrest. Refusing to assist with the implementation of a repugnant, albeit constitutional, act ("warrantable") is also "anti-commandeering". Therefore, how a State responds to an unconstitutional federal act indicates both its awareness of and its level of willingness to assert its sovereign, constitutional authority.

Convention of States or Nullification? (3/2014)

Questions: Is the sole remedy for restoring constitutional order an "Art V Convention of States" whose dual purpose is to fashion new amendments to curtail a runaway federal government as well as to clarify core constitutional principles which have been so terribly misconstrued and muddled over the years? Or is the vigorous State nullification of unconstitutional federal acts alone the way to go?

With these critical questions in mind, my biggest concern with an Art V Convention of States (COS) process alone is the length of time it will require--up to 20 years according to Mark Levin, a leading COS proponent--during which time much more federal mischief can be perpetrated against the States, the People and the Constitution--perhaps irremediably.

Other concerns about COS: Why should we believe that the feds will faithfully uphold new amendments created by COS any more faithfully than they have upheld current amendments or the original meaning and intent of core Constitutional principles? Also, who can feel assured that there are a sufficient number of reliable constitutionalists in State governments to ensure a prudent and responsible COS amendment process and outcome? And who of us is reasonably confident that the treachery of self-serving lobbyists will not corrupt the faithfulness of COS participants and the integrity of their handiwork? These questions inexorably lead to this critical question: Can any conscious patriot possibly believe that a COS process alone can save the Republic?

To my way of thinking, our pressing for assertive State nullification/ anti-commandeering actions while concurrently monitoring a well-focused and untainted Convention of States process is, very likely, the most efficacious and prudent way forward. After all, we should be able to walk and chew gum at the same time.

It is encouraging to note that the number of State anti-commandeering and nullification actions are increasing. (Check the 10th Amendment Center site for updated info on those actions.) Coupled with a growing number of States approving a COS, it clearly appears that many thoughtful Americans in State leadership positions are finally awakening to the threat of Progressive tyranny and finally committing themselves to remedial actions.

To further encourage the advancement of this two-pronged strategy to restore constitutional order, I believe a well-represented "Operation American Spring" occupation of DC beginning May 16th and the significant uptick in nullification/anti-commandeering activities already sweeping the country may well serve to throttle the ruthless Progressive assault on our political system and way of life. The blockbuster combo of nullification already in play and a successful "Operation American Spring" occupation of DC will, I believe, constitute the death knell of big-government Progressivism and restore constitutional order in these united States.

With so much frustration, defiance and resistance taking place at both the grassroots and State levels today, the political elites know that the fecal matter is about to hit the proverbial fan, and that the unstoppable force of millions will simply be too much for them to ignore or to easily sweep aside.

In truth, and for the first time, I believe America's ruling class and its corporate enablers are genuinely scared and, like cornered rats, are prepared to either appease the People's demands or, in their desperation, to suicidally confront an increasingly determined throng of American patriots. Either way, my sense is that stalwart American patriots will carry the day. I have to believe this, or accept the awful prospect of tyranny's triumph.

Postscript: the much-touted "Operation of American Spring" was a virtual bust. Patriots didn't show up--again!

On Civil Disobedience & Nullification

I have often alluded to civil disobedience and state nullification as preliminary remedies to federal usurpation, the ultimate remedies, of course, being that of secession and rebellion. And in these stubbornly uncertain times, I still find myself inexorably drawn to this subject's unsettling relevance. In truth, the importance of this subject can never be overstated and should never be ignored.

At a recent Monticello College-sponsored seminar, we were told that to restore constitutional order we must all actively participate in a "cultural transformation", meaning that the woes of American society fundamentally stemmed from a cultural--not political--breakdown; that a lack of personal virtue, faith in a higher power, and personal responsibility are the root causes of our social, economic and political malaise; that we must return to those core American principles which shaped who we once were as a people before the social engineers and neo-Marxists took over.

To achieve these transformational ends, the presenter made it clear that it was our individual responsibility to ensure that education--both home-schooling and public--should once again infuse our youth with the importance of free-market capitalism, personal and public virtue, personal responsibility, and "authentic ownership" of property versus ownership-by-credit; that an individual's passionate pursuit of a vocation vs a profession was much more productive and healthier for individuals, families and a free society than merely a dispassionate commitment to pursuing a lucrative career. It was explained that these virtues and values characterized those stellar men and women who founded our country in 1775 - 1787. And, of course, he made it clear that such a cultural transformation would not come easy and would require a substantial period of time and personal engagement to achieve.

Reflecting on his excellent commentary, my concern is that while we few can, indeed, plant the seeds of cultural rejuvenation--and we definitely should try—I fear that the smothering canopy of socialism which has so deeply perverted the very foundations of our once free and enlightened society will, despite our best efforts, prevent the timely germination of those rejuvenating seeds which will culminate in our society's suicide. So, my more assertive solution is to better ensure a rejuvenated free society by both affirmatively and assertively eliminating that toxic canopy. But, again, I feel that a rational personal philosophical justification for this more assertive approach to restoring and defending traditional American values is needed.

So, here's how I see the succession of steps required to achieve constitutional order and cultural transformation: active political and judicial engagement to resist overreach, followed by civil disobedience, tenacious nullification, secession and, if necessary, rebellion.

Though mindful that civil disobedience is the essence of constitutionalism, absent which there is no effective recourse but armed resistance, it is also clear that for disobedience to be effectual the freely and openly disobedient individual must be willing to bear the burden of legal sanctions, e.g. incarceration. Without the willingness to accept punishment for bucking injustice and corruption, one's effectively asserting civil disobedience to right a wrong perpetrated by government or other offending entity is impossible

As Martin Luther King, Jr. wrote from his Birmingham jail, *"I submit that an individual who breaks the law that his conscience tells him is unjust, and willingly accepts the penalty by staying in jail to arouse the conscience of the community over its injustice, is in reality expressing the very highest respect for law."* And so it is.

Notable examples of successful civil disobedience are the civil rights movement and women's suffrage, among others, which effectively served to remedy unconstitutional or otherwise unconscionable action or inaction on the part of government.

In his "Resistance to Civil Government" (1849), Henry David Thoreau underscored the preeminence of the individual in a civil society with these statements: "A government in which the majority rule in all cases cannot be based on justice; we should be men first and subjects afterward; there are nine hundred ninety-nine patrons of virtue to one virtuous man; a wise man will not leave the right to the mercy of chance, nor wish it to prevail through the majority; any man more right than his neighbors constitutes a majority of one; there will never really be a free and enlightened state until it comes to recognize the individual as a higher and independent power, from which all its own power and authority are derived, and treats him accordingly." Thus, he asserts the justification for civil disobedience when clear violations of the sanctity of the individual are perpetrated.

And since individuals are the essential elements of society, its culture, its communities and the states in which they dwell, it is not a big leap to rationally apply this truth to Americans and to the United States of America.

Regarding the so-called "Civil War", aka "War of Northern Aggression", though the southern States lost the war and, with the barrel of a Union gun to their heads, were compelled to accede to a forfeiture of their constitutional right to secede in the future, in truth they never really lost their inherent right to nullify or to secede. Why? Because, by definition, both are inherent and unalienable rights, and neither is prohibited by the Constitution. (It may be instructive to note that as a condition of their ratifying the US Constitution in 1788, Maryland, Rhode Island and Virginia reserved their right to secede, a claim which was never questioned by either thje framers or ratifiers. Surely, then, this inherent right cannot be logically denied to any state.)

As Sen. Henry Cabot Lodge writes, **"It is safe to say there was not a man in the country, from Washington and Hamilton to Clinton and Mason, who did not regard the new system as an experiment from which each and every state had a right to peaceably withdraw."**

And in an antebellum West Point textbook entitled "A View of the Constitution" written by Judge William Rawle, it is stated that "the secession of a State depends on the will of the people of such a State," again underscoring a state's inherent right to decide its political fate.

In his "Democracy in America", Alexis de Toqueville observed that "The Constitution of the United States was formed by the free will of the States; these, by uniting, did not lose their nationality or become fused in one single nation. If today one of those same States wishes to withdraw its name to the contract [which created the union], it would be hard to prove that it could not do so."

And as history has clearly shown, it was only by sheer weight of overwhelming military force that this inherent right was denied to the

Confederate States of America. (Note: it is for me revealing that no Confederate leader was brought to trial for treason after the war. I suspect the reason for this is that since a trial would have forced a verdict on the constitutional legality of secession, federal prosecutors wisely opted to conveniently circumvent that issue altogether. No sense losing in court what you think you may have won on the battlefield.)

Essentially, since secession is not explicitly addressed, nor is it specifically prohibited, in the US Constitution, the unity of the States is solely dependent upon the mutual benefits derived by both the federal government and individual state governments from that relationship.

In his "How to Resist Federal Tyranny in the 21st Century", Tom Woods states that "If you enter into a contract with somebody, never, ever would you say that the other party in the contract can exclusively interpret what it means...[when] the federal government has a monopoly on interpreting the Constitution ...they're going to interpret it in their own favor." This of course, applies to all branches of the federal government. In effect, like all contracts, both parties must have the inherent power to enforce the contract's provisions, failing which it ceases to be a contract but merely a means of asserting supremacy by one of the parties over the other.

Important to note is that Amendment IX declares that "the enumeration in the Constitution of certain rights shall not be construed to deny or disparage others retained by the people" and Amendment X states that "the powers not delegated to the United States are reserved to the states respectively or to the people." Thus, since the power to secede is not denied to them in the Constitution, it can be logically concluded that the States and the People have implicitly retained the inherent right to withdraw from the union. And since the federal government, which is inclusive of the Congress, the Executive and the Judiciary, is a party to the contract with the States, if the federal government were to overstep its Constitutional authority by exercising powers not specifically granted to it, short of open rebellion how else could unconstitutional federal acts be thwarted if not by nullification or secession? Without the means of escaping a broken contract, it would have to be assumed that the States and/or the People would be inherently willing to submit to any manner of federal overreach or tyranny. But since no reasonable person would think such was the framers' intention, nor believe that a free people would be so readily inclined to tolerate such servility, it fair to conclude that nullification and, indeed, secession, are the reserved and unalienable constitutional rights of the states and of the people, no less so than is rebellion itself.

Of course, short of secession, nullification, a well-grounded and peaceful Constitutional remedy, is the states' most efficacious and least disquieting defense against federal encroachment. We see this today in the number of states which have effectively nullified all manner of federal usurpations which have violated the people's trust and exceeded constitutional restraints on the federal government. And, of course, whether or not nullification is effective depends upon the tenaciousness of the nullifying state(s). If states routinely and submissively allow any of the branches of the federal government to overreach their constitutional authority, then nullification is but an untried theory.

However, as Thomas Jefferson said, "there is a rightful remedy to the federal government's uncontrollable quest for power. It's called nullification." So, while it's much more than theory, only the will of the states and the people can make it so. Nullification means invalidating and rendering null and void any executive edict/regulation, legislative mandate or judicial fiat emanating from DC which violates the constitutional contract between the states and the federal government. (Carefully note here that nullification should never be restricted just to legislative or executive overreach, but to judicial overreach as well.)

Without an effective balance of power between the states and the federal government as contracting parties, the framers fully understood that discord and disunity would be inevitable. Thus, Section 8 of the Constitution (enumeration of federal powers) and the Bill of Rights (the first ten amendments) were created by the states to clearly delineate respective powers in the contract, thereby striking that harmonious balance which would preclude disorder and disunion.

In the 18th century, Nathaniel Ames of Massachusetts observed, "The state governments represent the wishes and feelings of the people. They are the safeguards and ornament of our liberties--they will afford a shelter against the abuse of power, and will be the natural avengers of our violated rights." Well, that was the idea anyway.

Unfortunately, passage of the 17th Amendment seriously impaired the ability of states to check federal power. Effectively eliminating the framers' mechanism for ensuring the states' direct representation and influence in the Senate, for all intent and purposes the US of A, that well-crafted constitutional republic it was originally designed to be, was suddenly and unceremoniously transformed into an unwieldy representative democracy and the balance of power has, since then, dramatically shifted to the federal government. Repealing this ill-conceived amendment should be a top priority of the states.

And no discussion about nullification can ignore the "supremacy clause" (Art VI), the latter which is so relentlessly and mindlessly touted by modern liberal adherents who mistakenly believe that it constitutionally negates all state authority and any inherent state right to nullify or secede. Incredibly, what nullification detractors continue to conveniently and dishonestly ignore is the actual wording of the clause: "This Constitution, and the laws *which shall be made in pursuance thereof*...shall be the supreme law of the land." The clause in no way, shape or form unilaterally grants supremacy to the federal government in all matters of law, but only those laws enacted which fully comport with its enumerated powers. For all practical purposes, therefore, the states too, as parties to the constitutional contract, enjoy supremacy in their sphere of authority. Thus, in all cases it is within the implicit and expressed power of the states to determine whether or not a federal action is constitutional.

Finally, I have to say that every time I delve into this compelling subject I am unshakably convinced that civil disobedience, nullification and secession are absolute rights which no power on earth can rightfully deny us. And drawing upon the best minds in our history, my conclusion is inescapable: the only effectual means of ushering in a cultural renaissance in America and of restoring constitutional order is by enough Americans becoming actively engaged in changing the system from within, failing which we must be unyielding in our resistance to cultural and political stagnation even if it means nullification or even secession.

With nearly 46% of the electorate either functionally illiterate or simply brainwashed, our work is cut out for us. Going forward, there can be no compromising on constitutional principles with the Executive, the Congress and most certainly not with an increasingly renegade federal judiciary and bureaucracy upon which Progressives have so successfully relied to undermine the Republic. And with a GOP establishment habitually inclined to compromise the party's conservative principles, the challenge is all the greater.

To prevail and to reverse our society's headlong and irretrievable collapse into the quagmire of socialist tyranny, we must be fearlessly tenacious, assertive and true to ourselves and to the Constitution of the United States. Nothing else will work.

("Whenever the legislators endeavor to take away and destroy the property of the people, or to reduce them to slavery under arbitrary power, they put themselves into a state of war with the people, who are thereupon absolved from any further obedience." John Locke, 1690*)*

("A patriot must always be ready to defend his country against his government." Edward Abbey*)*

("If you will not fight for the right when you can easily win without bloodshed; if you will not fight when your victory will be sure and not too costly; you may come to the moment when you will have to fight with all the odds against you and only a precarious chance of survival. There may even be a worse case. You may have to fight when there is no hope of victory, because it is better to perish than to live as slaves." Winston Churchill*)*

("The preservation of the sacred fire of liberty and the destiny of the republican model of government are justly considered as deeply, perhaps as finally, staked on the experiment entrusted to the hands of the American people." George Washington, 1789*)*

("Whenever the people are well-informed, they can be trusted with their own government; whenever things get so far wrong as to attract their notice, they may be relied on to set them to rights." Thomas Jefferson, 1789*)*

("We are now trusting to those who are against us in position and principle, to fashion to their own from the minds and affections of our youth...This canker is eating on the vitals of our existence, and if not arrested at once, will be beyond remedy." Thomas Jefferson, 1821*)*

Federal Imperialism v State Sovereignty

For a painfully long time now, our federal masters and their judicial enablers have ignored and, to my way of thinking, flagrantly violated the Constitution with impunity. All too often, Supreme Court rulings have served to override common sense, constitutionality and original intent.

And so long as black-robed, unelected and unaccountable judicial oligarchs, aka judges, as well as the submissive states themselves allow "judicial supremacy" to trump "constitutional supremacy" on a whole host of consequential and foundational constitutional issues, our economic growth will be hobbled, our liberties diminished, state sovereignty degraded, constitutional order imperiled and common sense abandoned.

To wit, per Art 1.8.17 of the Constitution and provisions of the Northwest Ordinance of 1787, and despite a veritable cesspool of contrived and revisionist court rulings over the years through which I was barely able to wade, it appears glaringly obvious to me that our federal overseers are occupying millions of otherwise productive acres within the several states without the "concurrence" of those states and without constitutional justification.

Article 1.8.17 ("Enclave Clause") granted power to Congress "to exercise exclusive legislation in all cases whatsoever, over such district (not exceeding ten miles square) as may, by cession of particular states, and the acceptance of Congress, become the seat of the government of the United States [i.e. the District of Columbia], and to exercise like authority over all places purchased by the consent of the legislature of the state in which the same shall be for the erection of forts, magazines, arsenals, dockyards, and other needful buildings." Crystal-clear what the original meaning is here despite the shamelessly self-serving litany of subsequent spin on the part of our judicial overlords, the lap dogs of the federal government.

Clearly this clause meant that the people of the states empowered Congress to exercise complete jurisdiction and authority over all lands or facilities purchased within a state, provided it was with the consent of the legislature of that state, and that such lands would be used for the erection of forts, magazines, arsenals, dock yards, and other needful buildings." Clearly implied in this clause is that the several states, the immediate fiduciary agents of the people, reserve the right to restore state title to all lands within their borders which are not being used by the federal government for the specific and limited purposes provided in Art 1.8.17, that being "the erection of forts, magazines, arsenals, dock yards, and other needful buildings." Not a difficult concept, huh?

It is also important to note that nowhere in the Constitution is the federal government granted the enumerated power of complete jurisdiction and authority over state territory; thus, state retention and ownership of public lands stems from the 10th Amendment which reserves all rights to the states which are not specifically granted to Congress. The twisted and carefully crafted Delphic court rulings notwithstanding, the original meaning should be abundantly clear to all but the mentally afflicted.

Art 4.3.1 allowed a mechanism for the formation and admission of new states into the union, and Art 4.3.2 described the extent of congressional authority over federal territory within those states. Subsequently, the Supreme Court ruled that federal property applies only to the territory at the time of the Constitution's adoption and is considered public land only until that territory is granted statehood and the national debt incurred by the Revolutionary War is paid. In other words, temporary federal control over those lands.

In accordance with the Northwest Ordinance of 1787, which was re-enacted after the Constitution's ratification, all new states were to be admitted to the union on the basis of full equality with the original thirteen states. It was generally understood that as territories were granted statehood, the people of those states would acquire title to all lands within their state boundaries—except, of course, those lands granted to the feds for those well-defined purposes cited in Art 1.8.17.

To help pay down the national debt, Congress assured the states of full title to those lands not used for constitutionally sanctioned purposes when that land was sold off. The following then became the established policy for new states:

1. The feds would retain all ungranted public lands.

2. The feds guaranteed that it would dispose of these lands as soon as possible.

3. The new state would acquire jurisdiction over these lands as fast as they were sold to private individuals.

4. States would be admitted on the basis of "equal footing" with the original 13 states (each of which retained complete ownership/control over their respective territories.

As a result, all states east of the Mississippi and those comprising the Louisiana Purchase eventually acquired title to all but a very small portion of the land lying within their state boundaries.

However, following our war with Mexico, Congress inexplicably digressed from this policy and virtually eliminated the sale or disposal of federal lands in the western states. This resulted in Congress's retaining major portions of those state lands, this in direct contravention of the Constitution and of the Northwest Ordinance. Essentially, the federal government became the sole owner and manager of nearly 30%, or a whopping 650 million acres, of America's landmass, for the constitutionally unspecified purposes of maintaining national forests, national parks, national monuments, Indian reservations, coal and oil reserves, lands leased to farmers and ranchers, and resources-rich so-called "wilderness areas"--federal purposes which are not included in Art1.8.17. And, of course, the cost to taxpayers for maintaining these millions of acres and the Bureau for Land Management is in the billions of dollars.

Federal defenders of this overreach breathlessly point to the so-called "property clause" (Art 4.3.2) which provides that "Congress shall have power to dispose of and make any needful rules and regulations respecting the territory or other property belonging to the United States and any territory or property belonging to the United States." Clearly, doesn't this create a convenient constitutional ambiguity by contradicting the original intent of Art 1.8.17? Does this not exact restrictions on the western states, which had never been imposed on earlier states? So much for states being admitted into the union on "equal footing" and "full equality" with earlier states. Is federal retention of 30% of America's real estate really a "necessary and proper" exercise of federal powers? For anyone to believe this would require a willful suspension of common sense.

To give you a rough idea of how much state land is now imperially held by the feds, check this out: NV 85%, AL 70%, UT, 60%, OR 53%, AZ 47%, CA 45%, WY 42%, NM 42%, CO 37%, and poor Alaska 96%! Note: 65% of federal land holdings are located west of the Mississippi and <u>a paltry 1% of all federally controlled land in this country is currently being utilized for those specific purposes cited in Art 1.8.17</u>. One must wonder why these lands are still being held by the feds. Pay off the Revolutionary War debt? Gee, I don't think so. Lofty, if not entirely contrived, constitutional justifications? Or, more likely, the relentless federal grasp for power and, today, a way to placate a host of environmental allies by denying the states access to those God-awful climate-warming pollutants such as oil and gas.

Regarding the Enclave Clause, James Madison stated that "the public money expended on such places, and the public property deposited in them, require that they should be exempt from the authority of the particular State. Nor would it be proper for the places on which the security of the entire Union may depend to be in any degree dependent on a particular member of it. All objections and scruples are here also obviated by requiring the concurrence of the States concerned in every such establishment." But, have the courts sought the concurrence of the states? Nope.

Clearly, the federal government is occupying millions of acres without the "concurrence" of those states, but maintains their grip with the twisted and self-serving judicial sanction of federal Courts intent upon expanding and strengthening federal power.

So, what is the recourse of the several states? My opinion, which is shared by many other originalists, is that in keeping with the doctrine of state sovereignty, original intent and the 10th Amendment, states should simply legislatively assume title of all lands not being utilized by the federal government as specified in the Enclave Clause. Of course, to placate the courts and public opinion, states MIGHT want to first sue the federal government to acquire title. And since the states will not prevail in such a lopsided judicial struggle, they should then rightfully and unhesitatingly assert their 10th Amendment rights by immediately assuming direct ownership and control of what I have dubbed the "royal federal reserves" lying within their state boundaries.

But, do the chastened, weak-kneed, and heavily bribed states have the backbone to hazard the restoration of their constitutional sovereignty and honor? Ah, yes, that's the burning question.

The constitutional issue aside for a moment, in truth the achievement of energy independence alone should provide ample motivation for the states and their people to step up and take back their land, which is illegally held by the feds. And should the states fail to assert their rights under the original constitution, they should quietly accept their bondage and compliantly move on with their drab, submissive lives.

("In the Constitution, the term state most frequently expresses the combined idea...of people, territory and government. A state, in the ordinary sense of the Constitution, is a political community of free citizens, occupying a territory of defined boundaries, and organized under a government sanctioned and limited by a written constitution, and established by the consent of the governed." State of Texas v White, 1868*)*

*("Nothing should ever be implied as law which leads to absurd or unjust consequences. "*Abraham Lincoln, 1861*)*

Obamacare: Stop the Hand-Wringing & Nullify (12/2010)

Recently, two federal judges ruled in favor of Obamacare while a federal jurist in Virginia ruled against it. Huh? One must seriously question whether or not these guys are all reading the same Constitution I have before me.

In any event, I honestly cannot fathom nor can I abide all the needless hand-wringing and drama over the constitutionality of Obamacare. Of course it's not constitutional! Going forward then, exactly what's the most likely end game of the 20 or so Attorneys General who are suing the Administration over this latest federal intrusion in our lives?

First off, when our political system fails us, we should all remember that in the final analysis "we the people" are the final arbiters with respect to what is and what is not constitutional. Also, under the 9th and 10th Amendments, the States are implicitly within their constitutional authority to simply nullify any unconstitutional federal law, ruling or regulation. I won't mince words here: anyone who disputes this assertion either is not an objective student of the Constitution or of American history, or is driven by an alien ideological agenda altogether.

Moreover, the feds are supreme only insofar as their laws and rulings do not exceed their clearly defined enumerated powers. Thus, the expansive liberal view of "federal supremacy" is laid bare for all but the willfully blind and politically-motivated to easily see. As Alexander Hamilton asserted, the Supremacy Clause "expressly confines supremacy to laws made pursuant to the Constitution." That, of course, applies to both federal and state authority.

It should be routine that we always look to the Constitution and to the words of both the framers and the ratifiers for a clear, concise and accurate understanding of what properly constitutes Federal and State powers, a division of authority which was never intended by the framers to change over time. And reliance upon case law alone should NEVER, EVER be one's window on the original meaning and intent of the Constitution. Peering through that opaque window to determine original meaning merely results in further corruption and revisionism, thus further imperiling the framers' masterpiece of republican self-governance.

Happily for us all, understanding the clear meaning of the Constitution is NOT rocket science. If it were, we'd all have a convenient and pardonable defense for either not reading it, leaving it to others to interpret it for us, or simply violating it. Thus, we should all do ourselves and our country a favor and take the time to actually read the Constitution as well as the words of James Madison, Alexander Hamilton, Thomas Jefferson, George Mason, Benjamin Franklin and other framers whose wisdom and instructive commentary are as relevant today as they were when written. (And, again, don't forget that the ratifiers' debates are essential to achieving an uncorrupted and more complete understanding of the Constitution.)

As Thomas Jefferson wisely advised, "On every question of construction, let us carry ourselves back to the time when the Constitution was adopted, recollect the spirit manifested in the debates, and instead of trying to what meaning may be squeezed out of the text, or invented against it, conform to the probable one in which it was passed."

Thus, do we really need unelected black-robed "super legislators", a derisive term ascribed to Supreme Court jurists by fellow Justice Brandeis during the New Deal, telling us what any objective student of the Constitution already knows, that being that Obamacare, and more specifically the "individual mandate", is manifestly unconstitutional? No, not at all. So, why all the costly litigating and fuss? Frankly, it's insulting but, on a more sober note, it's also genuinely alarming. My concern here is that all this State-initiated litigation may be but a prelude to yet another surrendering of our liberties by the States. And if that's the unintended result of these Attorney Generals' action, then we should retire from the field of play and begin earnestly pushing for nullification and civil disobedience.

So, here are the big questions for me: if the Supreme Court imperiously rules against the States or the people on Obamacare--or on any other clear-cut constitutional issue--then what should the States do? Slavishly roll over and play dead yet once again, the Constitution and "we the people" be damned? Sadly, that's pretty much been their default inclination for the last 100+ years. But, alas, enough is enough!

In a word, self-imposed State servility must cease! If the Republic is to survive, the States must be fully prepared to interpose between the feds and the people of their states, thus restoring the proper co-equality of State and Federal authority. Nothing less can any longer be tolerated if the Republic is to survive.

At long last, constitutional order must be placed on a path to fullest restoration if we are to preserve the greatest achievement in self-government the world has ever known. Trite though it may sound, the States and "we the people" really do need to stand up if we are to see this constitutional restoration to fruition.

Finally, we should all carefully read the Constitution and INSIST that our State leaders defend our Constitutional rights, federal judicial circuses and insufferable overreach be damned. And if the States and the courts fail us yet again, then, of course, our founders unequivocally counseled that it is "we the people" who are duty-bound to "take such measures to redress the injury to the Constitution as the exigency may suggest and prudence justify." In other words, it is left to us to take appropriate action to restore constitutional order.

Timid hand-wringing in the face of judicial overreach is unacceptable, irresponsible and self-defeating.

10th Amendment:
The Commonsense Remedy to Federal Tyranny

Though I've carefully listened to and read his explanations, I remain utterly flummoxed by Mark Levin's implacable opposition to a States' right to invoke its 10th Amendment constitutional authority to defend its citizens from federal usurpations.

Having carefully researched our Founders' intentions with respect to the 9th and 10th Amendments, the notion that States are not permitted to defend their authority and their citizens from federal encroachments and outright lawlessness flies in the face of original intent and commonsense.

Dubbed by Thomas Jefferson the "rightful remedy" to federal usurpation, the meaning of the 10th Amendment is crystal-clear as to what a State's power is in this federal compact. "The powers not delegated [by the States/People] to the United States [the federal government] by the Constitution [Art 1 Sec 8], nor prohibited by it to the States, are reserved to the States respectively, or to the people."

Thus, any powers not specifically delegated to the central government by the Constitution are vested in the States and/or the People AND, similarly, any power not specifically prohibited to the States by the Constitution is vested in the States. Doesn't get clearer than that.

As for the grossly and often deliberately misinterpreted *Supremacy Clause*, carefully note that the Constitution, of the which the 9th and 10th Amendments are a part, is the Supreme Law of the land--NOT the Supreme Court or any other branch of the federal government, and, of course, most certainly not the States. (If, as many on the left irresponsibly proclaim, the feds are the supreme law of the land, then why have a Constitution at all? Why bother buttressing the notion that we are a republic? In all matters of law, let's simply submit to the central authority and be done with this republican charade.)

Note the carefully crafted wording of the *Supremacy Clause* (Art VI, Para 2): "This Constitution, and the Laws of the United States **WHICH SHALL BE MADE IN PURSUANCE THEREOF**, and all Treaties made, or which shall be made, under the Authority of the United States, shall be the supreme Law of the Land; and the Judges in every State shall be bound thereby, any Thing in the Constitution or Laws of any State to the contrary notwithstanding." Thus, the *Supremacy Clause* renders federal authority supreme ONLY insofar as the power exercised is within its clearly defined enumerated powers (Art 1 Sec 8). Please carefully re-read that provision. Commit it to memory. And never again permit a modern liberal, jurist or any other authoritarian to deliberately misinterpret or misquote this constitutional provision in order to advance his or her political agenda. Don't let them get away with it--ever!

Also, despite Mr. Levin's mystifying assertion to the contrary, objective research clearly demonstrates that James Madison, "father of the Constitution", did not debunk nullification. Not ever! In truth, Madison took exception not to nullification, but to South Carolina's assertion in 1832 that a State's nullifying a particular federal act/law would stand unless 3/4 of the States voted against that nullifying act. And, of course, that assertion is most certainly in error. That said, in his *Notes on Nullification* Madison did somewhat temper his enthusiasm for nullification, asserting that while nullification is "a natural right" and is "extra-constitutional" that, as a last resort, it should be invoked but only when there is "insupportable oppression." Clearly concerned about the viability of the union at the time he didn't define what constituted "insupportable oppression", leaving that definition to the individual States themselves. But, again, even in his twilight years when he was genuinely concerned about the union breaking up he did not de-legitimatize the nullification remedy at all. In short, on this score Mr. Levin is dead wrong!

And this is also well-worth remembering: like nullification and a whole host of other residual powers not specifically enumerated as State powers or specifically prohibited to the States, secession too is NOT prohibited to the States by the Supreme Law of the Land, that being the CONSTITUTION.

I realize that the confusion--deliberate, inadvertent or otherwise--on this subject stems from a terribly misguided and revisionist education or political predilection which advances a nationalist and/or statist philosophy and viewpoint, but the Constitution means what it says, and not what some would like it to mean.

In a nutshell, what all this means is that State nullification of executive orders, federal laws, Supreme Court rulings and bureaucratic regulations which do not comport with the supreme Law of the Land, that being the Constitution, is, hands down, THE wisest, most credible and most effective remedy.

Finally, though we've been conditioned to believe that the Supreme Court is the final arbiter on all matters of law, for God's sake read the Constitution, the applicable Federalist Papers and Ratifying documents. It will then become abundantly clear that We the People are the final arbiters of what is and what is not constitutional--not the Supreme Court! And not one of our Founders would take exception to that foundational assertion.

"To consider the judges as the ultimate arbiters of all constitutional questions [is] a very dangerous doctrine indeed, and one which would place us under the despotism of an oligarchy."--Thomas Jefferson

Tragically, most States are populated by politicians who are ignorant of the Constitution or who reside in States which have been bought off and intimidated by federal largess. And while there has been an extraordinary level of nullification sweeping the country of late, much more needs to be done by the States to restore their co-equality with the central government, failing which the remedy lies clearly on the shoulders of We the People. Will we opt for peaceful nullification or something else too awful to contemplate?

Finally, despite all the preceding revisionist case law and gratuitous political-driven interpretations of the Constitution, we've got to get this right! Let the ratified Constitution ALWAYS be our guide!

("The powers delegated by the proposed Constitution to the federal government are few and defined. Those which are to remain in the State governments are numerous and indefinite. The former will be exercised principally on external objects, as war, peace, negotiation, and foreign commerce; with which last the power of taxation will, for the most part, be connected. The powers reserved to the several States will extend to all the objects which, in the ordinary course of affairs, concern the lives, liberties, and properties of the people, and the internal order, improvement, and prosperity of the State." --James Madison, Federalist No. 45)*

[6] THE UNION & SECESSION

The Myth of American Indivisibility

No nation is immutable. Historically, nations evolve and devolve. And there's no historical precedent which would justify the assertion that America, as currently constituted, will be an exception to this rule.

And though our Founders had hoped their carefully crafted Constitution which created a federal republic would remain intact in perpetuity, none deluded themselves into believing that, for better or for worse, the inherent depravity and corruptibility of man wouldn't--inevitably and likely irretrievably--alter both the nature and structure of American society and government. Thus, from a historical perspective, the reconstruction of our society and its model of governance is inescapable.

Today, there is a degenerative ideological struggle for the very soul of our nation, both political and cultural. The increasingly acrimonious contention between big government (centralization of authority) and small government (decentralization of authority) proponents has led to a deeply divided American citizenry along what may be accurately described as statist/socialist and constitutionalist/capitalist lines. In truth, political, economic and cultural indications clearly suggest that this ideological divide is most likely irreconcilable. But, take heart. This in no way pre-ordains a bloody clash of arms for these "united States" to peacefully and satisfactorily accommodate the historical imperative for change. Although secession is no longer merely a remote possibility, what shape the re-ordering of this union takes is anyone's guess.

But, first, let's very briefly examine the enduring myth that secession is illegal, unconstitutional, treasonous, or otherwise constitutionally prohibited.

Not even Daniel Webster, a particularly ardent nationalist, could prove that the Constitution was anything but a *compact*, aka contract, among the States and their creation, the federal government, requiring all parties to that contract to abide by the terms of the clearly defined terms of that contract. And as has always been the case, when a party to a contract violates the terms of that contract, that contract null and void.

We need but to look to history to understand that even at its inception and early development, liberty-loving Americans have never been of one mind. Just as the thirteen colonies individually abolished their political bands with England, eventually acceding to confederation and, subsequently, to a "more perfect" constitutional federal union, a nationalist would, indeed, be sorely challenged to prove that any of the States ever freely, knowingly or contractually surrendered or otherwise delegated their fundamental rights as sovereign entities to an omnipotent, overarching national government. Quite the contrary. Representatives of the original 13 colonies, which had individually agreed to secede from British rule, eventually fashioned a constitutional federal system of governance which painstakingly incorporated the core unifying principle of state-federal co-equality and dual sovereignty in a constitutionally balanced federal system of governance.

In the *Treaty of Paris* (1783) which concluded the Revolutionary War, Britain explicitly recognized the independence and sovereignty of *each* of her 13 former colonies as did the American delegates who signed the treaty. Thus, from the outset, and most certainly during the drafting and ratification of the constitution, state sovereignty and the core principle of co-equality were enshrined with nary a word of protest or disagreement on the part of the framers, ratifiers or from the people themselves.

Since ratification of the Constitution in 1787, North Carolina and Rhode Island being the last States to join the union in 1790, Americans have been buffeted by threats of and movements toward secession in the north, south, east and west--**NOT**, as revisionists would have us believe, just in the south.

State nullification of federal laws and civil disobedience have characterized America's experiment in constitutional self-government since its inception. Though the _War for Southern Independence_ in 1861 - 1865, erroneously characterized by revisionist historians as the "Civil War", seemed to have put an end to the notion that the several states "are and of right ought to be free" of unconstitutional constraints on their liberties by virtue of their co-equal status in the union, nullifying federal overreach has become as commonplace today as it was before the War of Southern Secession, aka War of Northern Aggression. In fact, as the ideological divide has sharpened in recent years, state resistance to federal encroachment has become more pervasive and assertive than even before 1861. (Just type _nullification anti-commandeering_, or _secession in the USA_ in your browser. Or go to the 10th Amendment Center for a comprehensive examination of historical and contemporary nullification actions. You'll be astounded by the number of serious anti-commandeering and nullification actions in play today.)

Even Abraham Lincoln, often conveniently convoluted on the subject of secession and the sanctity and inviolability of the union, posited on the floor of Congress in 1847 that _"any people, anywhere, being inclined and having the power, have the right to rise up and shake off the existing government, and form a new one that suits them better. This is a most valuable, a most sacred right, a right which we hope and believe is to liberate the world."_ And in his 1861 Inaugural Address, he proclaimed that _"whenever the people shall grow weary of the existing government, they can exercise their constitutional right of amending it or their revolutionary right to dismember or overthrow it."_ So much for indivisibility in perpetuity. Not even the pre-eminent "one nation, indivisible" advocate himself believed that bunkum.

Logically, since secession was never in any way prohibited under the constitution, under the 10th Amendment, therefore, States have clearly reserved the right to secede from the union. In fact, contingent upon their ratification of the Constitution, and without any voices of objection raised by either the Framers or other states, Virginia, New York and Rhode Island explicitly reserved their right to secede, i.e. to reassume those powers granted to the federal government, should their sovereign rights be violated by the latter. (Note: Virginia cited its conditional ratification of the Constitution itself as a legal basis for her subsequent _Ordinance of Secession_.)

As H. Newcomb Morse points out in the **Stetson Law Review**, "because the Constitution did not forbid secession, then every state <u>acceding</u> to the Constitution had the implied right of <u>seceding</u> from it" as well. To wit, the 10th Amendment clearly stipulates that *"the powers not delegated to the United States by the Constitution, <u>nor prohibited by it to the States,</u> are reserved to the States respectively, or to the people."* Thus, it is slam-dunk obvious to all but the hardened big government nationalists that nullification and secession remain perfectly constitutional and anything but treasonous.

Further, in the **Madison Papers**, <u>James Madison observed that implicit in the contractual relationship between the states and the federal government</u> *<u>"a breach of any one article by any one party [to this contract], leaves all other parties at liberty to consider the whole convention as dissolved."</u>* Thus, if the Founders intended the union to be legally indissoluble, would not the Framers and Ratifies have specifically included that prohibition in the Constitution? Of course.

And given that the northern armies were withdrawn from southern states only after those states had each been compelled to incorporate into their constitutions a clause specifically <u>relinquishing</u> their inherent right to secede in the future, a reasonable person must logically conclude that the *inherent* right of secession remains intact, and that only with a gun barrel to their heads did those states relinquish what is still an inviolable and inherent constitutional right. <u>Like, how could the states surrender a right unless they had it in the first place?</u> Also, were any leaders of the defeated Confederacy tried for treason by the victorious North? Nope! As Gene Kizer noted in his **Right of Secession**, *<u>"there were no treason trials against former Confederates because any one trial would likely prove the legal right of secession, and eminently practical Northerners were not about to lose in a court of law what they had won on the battlefield."</u>*

Thomas Jefferson's <u>Kentucky Resolution of 1798</u> reaffirmed state sovereignty and the absolute right of the states to determine for themselves when the Constitution which embodies the state-federal contract is violated by the federal government. In short, Jefferson observed that *"the several States composing the United States of America, are not united on the principle of unlimited submission to their General Government."* And in his draft Declaration of Protest in 1825, Jefferson noted that while the states greatly valued the *"blessings of their Union"* that *"they would, indeed, consider such a rupture as among the greatest calamities which could befall them; but not the greatest. There is yet one greater, submission to a government of unlimited powers."*

Without specifically reviewing the litany of American nullification and secessionist activities here, the reader is encouraged to research, among others, the following nullification and secessionist events in our country's history: New England's Hartford Convention which set New England on the course of secession, precluded only by the sudden conclusion of the War of 1812; the Tariff Compromise of 1833 which merely delayed the inevitable constitutional showdown between the South and the North; nullification by ten northern states of the Fugitive Slave Laws of 1850; the Kentucky and Virginia Resolutions of 1798 authored by Jefferson and Madison respectively in opposition to the Alien and Sedition Acts, etc.........

In the Constitutional Convention of 1787, the word "accede" (agree to), which is the opposite of the word "secede", was liberally used to describe the legal relationship between the States and the Union. And to short-circuit any specious argument that the Constitution was not a co-equal compact between the States and the federal government, these quotes from James Madison himself:

"That this assembly doth explicitly and peremptorily declare that it views the powers of the federal Government as resulting from the compact, to which the States are parties." (Virginia Resolutions of 1798)

"[The Constitution is] a compact among the States in their highest sovereign capacity." (Madison's ltr to Mr. Everett in 1830)

Some have and will continue to desperately advance the argument that the preamble of the Constitution speaks about "We the People" as the forgers of the Constitution, thus undermining the compact argument, the latter which forms the legal basis for the right of a state's withdrawal from the union. In fact, the Constitution was, indeed, ratified by the people of each state, **BUT** in special State constitutional conventions and not directly by the people. Thus, it is obvious that the Constitution was not ratified (acceded to) by a referendum of the general American population of a non-existent supreme nation state. In fact, the use of the words "We the People" in the preamble was necessitated by the practical reality of the Framers not being able to accurately predict which of the States would eventually accede (join) and which would not. Thus, listing the individual sovereign states in the preamble as parties to the union *before* all States actually acceded was impractical and a source of possible embarrassment. In fact, had the Convention listed the States and all but one acceded, then the Constitution and "union" would have been invalid owing to an absence of unanimity. Thus, the Constitution applied only to those states which ratified it which, at the time of George Washington's inauguration, consisted of only eleven of the thirteen States. <u>Implicit then is the fact that from the outset States were not and could not be coerced into joining the union</u>. Thus, ratification was a strictly voluntary process and the framers never delegated authority, either explicitly or implicitly, to the federal government or to any of the other states to coerce individual states into joining or remaining in the union.

An astute and highly regarded student of American democracy, Alex de Tocqueville, in his **Democracy in America**, observed that *"the union was formed by the <u>voluntary agreement</u> of the States; and in uniting together they have not forfeited their nationality, nor have they been reduced to the condition of one of the same people. <u>If one of the States chooses to withdraw from the compact, it would be difficult to disprove its right of doing so, and the Federal Government would have no means of maintaining its claims directly either by force or right.</u>"*

That said, what most folks don't know and precious few historians will tell them is that the South did not simply awaken one morning and heedlessly gallop headlong into a glorious, rebel-yelling War of Secession merely to keep slaves in bondage. Not at all. Secession was carefully debated and some of the greatest legal minds of the day were engaged in those debates.

Of singular importance in the South's decision to peacefully withdraw from the union--and only with the consent of the citizens in each state--was the conveniently overlooked fact that for decades the onerous federal taxation of the South had effectively retarded the South's industrial development, thus arguably ensuring its prolonged dependence upon slave-based agriculture. To wit, upwards of 70% of all federal taxes were paid by 6 million Southerners, nearly all of which was spent in the

North and West where nearly 20,000,000 citizens resided! Clearly, a disproportionate and unconstitutional burden on the South.

Also, for years high-minded Northern Abolitionists actively and illegally aided and abetted slave revolts in the south which resulted in considerable insecurity and tumult, raising Southern fears of rape and massacre. Southerners were all too mindful of the terrible slaughter of white colonists in Haiti and were genuinely fearful of such a scenario playing out in their own communities.

Of fundamental importance too is the fact that the wealthier North which relied upon a captive Southern market to sustain its prosperity was averse to allowing the South to peacefully withdraw from an increasingly unproductive and economically strangulating union with the North. Thus, though reluctant to make the break, the South, feeling itself victimized and bereft of reasonable options, could no longer rationally justify its remaining in the union at any cost. And, of course, that was their right then, and it remains the constitutional right of all states today.

And this extremely important point: though Art 1.10 of the Constitution reads, in part, "No State shall enter into any Treaty, Alliance or Confederation...without the consent of Congress", as a practical matter the southern States did not violate this article in 1861 because they hadn't confederated or allied themselves with one another until AFTER each had separately seceded from the Union. Only after they had each legally withdrawn from the union did they individually opt to become members of a new political union, that being the Confederate States of America.

So, whether the revisionists and nationalists like it or not, both nullification and secession are completely legal and respected constitutional principles. In fact, the principle of secession is enshrined in our Declaration of Independence which justified the colonies' secession from England. Clearly, our Founders would solidly espouse the view that if nullification were to fail to safeguard individual liberty, constitutional order and the rule of law, then secession, among other unalienable remedies, would be a legitimate and lawful remedy.

Back now to America's transformation and our path forward.

When in the 50's Nikita Khruschev warned that the Soviet Union and Communism would "bury" the USA and the West, he was only half right. I believe that the American union <u>as we know it</u> is being "buried", but it is Americans themselves who are doing the shoveling and the Progressives/Modern Liberals who are facilitating the process.

Since the advent of Progressivism over a century ago, America's socialist transformation has been underway. What the Soviets couldn't accomplish by bluster and intimidation, Progressives have been cleverly achieving with surprising success and rapidity. But, not all Americans have been content with that conversion.

Greatly contributing to the accelerating political and cultural polarization in the country is the current President's tactical reliance on racial politics and class warfare to further exacerbate those societal divisions necessary to "fundamentally transform the United States of America" into a welfare state which, to most Americans, is utterly repellent.

In a persuasive article appearing on the *FactsNotFantasy* blog, author Alan Caruba succinctly summarizes the accelerated makeover Obama and his predecessors have been perpetrating. To wit, the federal government has seized control of one-sixth the nation's economy by "asserting control over the provision of healthcare"; the administration seized control of GM and Chrysler "arbitrarily casting aside the rightful expectations of their bondholders and other creditors"; the administration is favorably considering a UN treaty "that would render the Second Amendment null and void"; the administration has sued AZ for enacting an immigration law that mirrors its own and has joined legal forces with foreign countries to similarly sue AZ and other states who are attempting to stem the tide and cost of illegal immigration; the FCC continues to assert its control over the internet despite a court order to cease and desist; and the explosion of an overreaching and extremely costly federal empire of agencies with "no legitimate basis in the Constitution" has become the order of the day (Dept. of Education, EPA, Dept. of Energy, BLM, to name a few).

And as the big government tide continues with breathtaking speed, grassroots and state-level pushback has begun in earnest. Nullification and secessionist movements are growing in support and strength, and both options are now regarded by many thoughtful, law-abiding Americans as perfectly legitimate and even inevitable.

If Americans cannot soon reverse the authoritarian tide and return to their constitutional and republican roots, the slide toward disunity is most certainly irreversible.

Finally, being inevitable in the human experience, change should not necessarily be feared or stubbornly resisted. If the cultural and political changes serve to safeguard the liberty, security and happiness of a society, then it should be embraced. However, should the changes occasion a reckless disregard for individual rights and the individual pursuit of happiness, then it is up to "we the people" to re-direct the course of events. **But, unity simply for the sake of unity is hollow and fraught with peril.** The challenge, then, is to either 1) forge a workable and peaceful division of the union which would safeguard and enhance state and regional self-determination, 2) fully re -establish federalism as originally intended by our Founders, this to preserve our political unity while fully restoring federal-state co-equality, or 3) secession. The only other choice is for us to rebel or to quietly acquiesce to an authoritarian national government.

What shape the eventual political and geographic re-ordering takes is completely in our hands, and that is precisely where it should be. And given the November 2012 election outcome as well as the threatening national lurch to the left, the shape of things to come may be clarified sooner than any of us might ever have imagined.

Am I advocating secession? Well, I can be dissuaded, but only if constitutional order is fully restored—and soon! In any event, free men must always keep their options open if they wish to remain free.

("We hold these truths to be self-evident, that all men are created equal, that they are endowed by their Creator with certain unalienable Rights, that among these, are Life, Liberty and the pursuit of Happiness. That to secure these rights, Governments are instituted among Men, deriving their just Powers from the consent of the governed. That, whenever any form of Government becomes destructive of these ends, it is the Right of the people to alter or to abolish it, and to institute new Government, laying its foundation

on such Principles, and organizing its powers in such form, as to them shall seem most likely to effect their Safety and Happiness...But when a long train of abuses and usurpations, pursuing invariably the same Object, evinces a desire to reduce them under absolute Despotism, it is their right, it is their duty, to throw off such Government, and to provide new Guards for their future Security." Declaration of Independence, July 4, 1776)

("The several States composing the United States of America, are not united on the principle of unlimited submission to the General Government." Thomas Jefferson, Kentucky Resolutions, 1798)

("It should be remembered that the founders, by their own actions, showed that they considered liberty more precious than unity." Robert F. Hawes, Jr. One Nation, Indivisible? 2006)

("The ultimate authority, no matter where any of its derivatives may be found, resides in the People alone." Thomas Jefferson)

Revisiting Secession:
A Constitutional Check on Federal Tyranny

Regarding the nature of this hallowed union of States, Americans must never, ever forget how the Founders viewed this union and the States which comprise it.

We must get past the adolescent, uninformed, politically correct and self-destructive notion that this union is inviolably indissoluble. <u>This union is not indivisible and never has been</u>. To believe otherwise defies history, logic, commonsense and flies in the face of our founders' understanding. Despite the relentless brainwashing over the years, a little honest research—without the blinders—is all that is required for readers to clearly understand the unassailability of a State's right to secede.

From its inception, the *United States of America* has been a *voluntary* association of sovereign States. In truth, no States were coerced to become members of that association. The union is a contractual association, a compact of independent sovereign States, any of which may secede from that association should the other party to that contract, that being the federal government, fails to uphold its contractual obligations.

To illustrate this point, as a condition of their ratifying the US Constitution, Virginia, New York and Rhode Island explicitly reserved their right to secede, and no objections from the Founders were raised. And, in accordance with the 10[th]Amendment, because the Constitution does not prohibit secession, that power like all other powers not specifically delegated to the federal government or specifically denied to the States, is indisputably reserved to the States.

No amount of revisionist history, nationalism, lawyerly contrivances, political obfuscation, or otherwise misguided case law can nullify that fundamental truth. No branch of the federal government is sovereign and supreme. The States and their citizens, the creators of the federal government, are sovereign and supreme, and that is the way our founders intended it to be.

Further, without the approval of a duly-elected State legislature or, should it be impossible to timely convene the legislature, an invitation of the

Governor, may force of arms be applied by either the federal government or sister States to quell rebellion within a particular State or to otherwise impose the union's will on any member of that compact. Because a misapplication of military force against a State or States may have been perpetrated in the past can in no way render that action lawful or constitutional today or in the future.

To be specific, Article IV, Sec 4 of the U.S. Constitution provides that "The US shall guarantee to every State in this Union a republican form of government." As such, it provides that the federal government shall protect each of the States of the union "against invasion, and on application of the legislature, or of the governor (when the legislature cannot be timely convened) against domestic violence."

Extremely important to note is the admonition of James Madison respecting this federal guarantee: in Federalist 43, he stated that the authority of the federal union *"extends no further than to a guaranty of a republican form of government"…and that "whenever the States may choose to substitute other republican forms, they have a right to do so."*

Conveniently overlooked by "nationalists", proponents of a supreme central government, is the fact that during the Constitutional Convention in 1787, James Madison, father of the Constitution, expressed his revulsion with the notion of the federal government's committing armed force against any State for any reason outside that limited purpose clearly provided for in Art IV, Sec 4, asserting that "a Union of States containing such an ingredient seemed to provide for its own destruction," saying that "the use of force against a State would look more like a declaration of war" and, to the party being assailed, "would probably be considered as a dissolution of all previous compacts by which it was bound [to the union}."

Thus, again, the only instance when the States or the federal authority may use force of arms against a State is if that State violates Art IV Sec 4 of the Constitution, a provision which mandates that all State governments be republican in design. And only if a foreign entity has seized control of that State's republican apparatus, thus rendering the legislature or the governor be something other than duly-elected or duly-authorized by its citizenry, may the States and/or the federal government apply military force to bring that State back into compliance with the Constitution.

That said, with the acquiescence of Congress, it is manifestly obvious that Pres. Lincoln, for whatever reason, political or otherwise, grossly exceeded his constitutional authority by committing armed forces against the seceding Confederate States of America in 1861, plunging this nation into one of the bloodiest, costliest and entirely avoidable wars in its history. And only by force of arms and a gun to their heads did the victorious North illegally compel the vanquished southern States to officially repudiate their inherent constitutional right to secede--which begs the question that if the States did not have the residual and inherent authority to secede then why would they be required to renounce that authority?

Asserting that the union was somehow indivisible, a concocted notion entirely foreign to the Founders, Mr. Lincoln, with much patriotic fervor, political fanfare, lofty rhetoric, and faulty argumentation, brazenly flouted the constitution with impunity by violating the sacred right of those southern States to legally secede from this voluntary union. In truth, the Founders well-understood that this union of States was never intended to be any more perpetual, aka eternal, than the confederation of States which preceded it, and that the union's survival was solely dependent upon the parties to the compact fully upholding their obligations under that contract.

It should be remembered that when any suggestion of calling forth military force against a State was brought up in the Constitutional or State Ratifying Conventions, the notion of indivisibility was unanimously rejected by both framers and ratifiers alike. Irresistible and unavoidable conclusion: by plunging the union into war with the Confederate States of America, our childhood hero, Abraham Lincoln, was in clear violation of the original meaning and intent of the Constitution. In short, Mr. Lincoln was dead wrong and our history teachers and textbooks have routinely and ignorantly foisted the myth of indivisibility upon generations of gullible children.

In all of my research over the years, there has never been any evidence that the myopic notion of union at any price was ever conceived of or in any way embraced by the Founders. In fact, there's a preponderance of evidence that the Founders viewed the very concept of indivisibility as dangerous. The States' inherent rights to secede, to interpose, and to resist an overreaching central government remain as unmistakable, unambiguous and unalienable today as they were in 1787.

For future reference, let that truth sink in. To safeguard individual liberty, constitutional governance, and the sovereignty of the States, the immediate fiduciary agents of We the People, if our resistance to tyranny must necessarily entail secession, then that rightful form of resistance must be fully embraced and fearlessly acted upon.

If the clear choice is liberty or union, can there be any doubt as to a free people's choice? Of course not. And the Founders knew that very well.

("It is plain a thing as possibly can be, that Congress can have no power but what we expressly give them." Archibald Maclaine, NC ratifying convention, 1788)

("Every power, Jurisdiction and Right, which is not by the said Constitution clearly delegated to the Congress...or to the departments of the Government... remains to the People of the several States, or to their respective State Governments to whom they may have granted the same." New York State Notice of Ratification, 1788)

Some Advice to "Secession Petitioners" (11/2012)

Historically, short of revolution or rebellion, secession is the ultimate practical check on centralization.

No branch of the federal government is empowered to decide upon the merits of a State's inherent right to secede. By its very nature, secession is an anti-federal act not requiring federal sanction.

Petitioning the federal government for *permission to secede* is self-contradictory and has no basis in English common law or American constitutional history. Secession, aka rescission or withdrawal, is a unilateral action and is not dependent upon mutual agreement between the parties to that contract.

Bottom line: when one enters into a contract and the other party violates that contract, does one request permission of the offending party to withdraw from that contract already violated? Of course not. <u>All compacts are subject to the equitable remedy of rescission in the event of a breach of contract.</u> It's really common sense and basic contract law. It's that straightforward.

At its inception, the US of A was a *voluntary* compact (contract) of *sovereign* States, each retaining the inherent authority to rescind its contractual relationship with the federal government, the other party to that contract, should the latter violate the terms of that contract/compact. That contractual relationship hasn't changed, though the misnamed "civil war" may have led us to believe otherwise. (By the way, "civil war" means that two or more factions are militarily struggling over control of the central government; however, in America's so-called "civil war", the South was defending its sovereign territory, not entertaining the capture and control of the central government in DC or of Northern territories.)

Force of arms alone by a revisionist, self-contradictory, union-at-any-price nationalist, that being our heretofore venerated Abe Lincoln, cannot--and did not--invalidate a State's inherent right to secede, or to otherwise rescind its ratification of this constitutional contract, no more than the federal government can legally or constitutionally annul the People's right to rebel in the face of tyranny.

Note: if secession were treasonous, which some maintained it was, why then were not southern leaders dragged into court following the North's successful invasion of the Confederate States of America? Easy. **Because the North didn't want to lose in court what they thought they had won on the battlefield.**

Fact: Perpetual union at any price was never contemplated or embraced by the Founders. Rebellion, secession, nullification, civil disobedience have remained core elements of America's republican fabric, and the threat or application of force on the part of the federal government cannot eradicate those foundational, inherent and unalienable rights of a free people.

When ratifying the Constitution, and only to the extent that it delegated certain of its sovereign powers to the federal government, not once did any State surrender its sovereignty. All powers voluntarily granted by the States to the federal government were very limited and very specific. All other powers, not specifically delegated by the States to the federal government remained with the States. The 10th Amendment enshrined that principle in the Constitution and, in so doing, reasserted the foundational principle that the federal government cannot unilaterally redefine the limits of its powers. To join the union, the States were not compelled to surrender anything, much less their sovereignty. Those few and specific State powers delegated to the federal government were granted freely and willingly on the understanding that both parties were obliged to fully comply with the covenant.

And remember, we not only seceded from England, but also, one by one, from the Articles of Confederation (which was said to be "perpetual") in order to form a "more perfect union" of States, a federal union which was comprised of but 11 of the original 13 states when George Washington was inaugurated on April 30, 1789 as the republic's first chief executive. NC and RI didn't ratify the Constitution and voluntarily join (*accede to*) the union until November 1789 and August 1790 respectively.

This "more perfect union"--MORE perfect, NOT perfect--was not intended nor expected to exist in perpetuity, but, like the Articles of Confederation, only until such time that the compact outlived its usefulness, no longer served the sovereign interests of the state(s), or until the parties to that contract violated its terms.

Studious historians, our Founders were not stupid men and well understood the corruptibility of men and all that man may devise. While they hoped the union would be strong, free and productive, they did not view secession and dissolution as ill-conceived, treasonous or unanticipated. We've just been brainwashed into believing that secession and dissolution are vile, wrong, corrupt and treasonous. Not so at all. If that were true, then our Founders were charlatans and short-sighted fools. They weren't.

All that said, as a first step I recommend that States opt for **nullification**, the "rightful remedy" as Jefferson described it, to resist unconstitutional acts by the Supreme Court, the Congress, the Chief Executive and their myriad bureaucracies which now comprise the unofficial fourth branch of government. And to render nullification more efficacious, States should enact punitive laws to prohibit the enforcement of those federal acts nullified by the State. This is called "interposition", or a State's insinuating itself between intrusive federal authority and the citizens of the State. Interposition would actually require the arrest, trial and imprisonment of any State OR federal agent who attempts to enforce a nullified federal act. Of course, implicit in nullification is the threat of secession should an invasive federal government fail to retreat within contractual parameters. But, again, secession is not by its nature treasonous or unavoidably violent. Not at all.

Finally, while I sincerely appreciate the wave of secessionist sentiment sweeping the country, secession, a serious constitutional matter, requires a majority of a State's residents to support the act. Anything less than a majority constitutes a protest and nothing more. And even with a majority expressing its support for secession, the people's State representatives must be won over as well, this if the label of "insurrection" and the invocation of Art I Sec 8 Para 15 are to be avoided.

Note: per Art IV Sec 4 of the Constitution, "on application of the Legislature, or of the Executive (when the Legislature cannot be convened)", the feds can be asked to intervene, whether that intervention is morally repugnant or not. Secession is a political act, not merely a feel-good act. Thus, on the subject of secession, both the people of a State and their duly elected State representatives must be in majority agreement on the issue of secession.

The million or so fearful and irate citizens who petitioned the White House in 2012 to grant their states permission to secede was therapeutic perhaps, but without any basis in commonsense or constitutional law.

("The source of Lincoln's power was his willingness to exercise power not grounded in the original Constitution but in his creative abilities to undermine the Constitution while rhetorically defending it." Donald Livingston, "Rethinking the American Union...")

("The secession of a state from the Union depends on the will of the people of such state. The people alone, as we have already seen, hold the power to alter their constitution." William Rawles, 1825*)*

("Each State, in ratifying the Constitution, is considered as a sovereign body, independent of all others, and only to be bound by its own voluntary act. In this relation then, the new Constitution will, if established, be a federal, and not a national constitution." James Madison, *The Federalist #39*, 1/16/1788*)*

(Whether we remain in one confederacy, or form into Atlantic, Mississippi confederacies, I believe not very important to our happiness." Thomas Jefferson, 1803*)*

[7] THE COURTS

Judicial Tyranny & We the People (10/2012)

With Obama's re-election in 2012, very liberal justices will be appointed to fill at least two vacancies, one of whom may be Justice Scalia, a fairly faithful conservative jurist.

Can you imagine the damage done should two more Kagans or Sotomayors be appointed? With the judiciary in his back pocket, Obama's "fundamental transformation of the United States" might well prove to be a fairly leisurely cakewalk.

But, not so fast!

First, for the libs to take over SCOTUS, the Senate would have to remain in Progressive hands, an unsettling prospect which diminishes with each unemployment report and blazing American consulate. For that reason alone, patriots had best pull out all stops to ensure a Republican/Tea Party takeover of the Senate in 2014.

That said, I am always flummoxed and sometimes mildly amused when I hear patriots feverishly warning against and whining about a liberal takeover of the Supreme Court, asserting that a liberal-dominated court will inevitably result in more socialism and authoritarianism.

Well, in truth, with or without a liberal majority on the bench, the judicial world as we now know it isn't much to celebrate.

Over the years liberal justices have done incalculable harm, even more so than self-described "conservative" judges. Years of faulty and revisionist case law, to which both schools have often been a party, is ample proof of the harm already perpetrated by a runaway judiciary inconsistently faithful to the original meaning and intent of the Constitution.

But let's not forget that OUR permitting the States to routinely rely on the federal judiciary to equitably settle constitutional disputes *with the federal government* (a surefire recipe for disaster), and OUR allowing the courts to imperiously overrule State voter referendums, thus imposing THEIR own will on the people in each State, have also materially contributed to the breakdown in constitutional order. So, who's really at fault? What is the proximate cause of this breakdown in constitutional order? WE ARE! Overweening liberal judges are merely a symptom of OUR failure. And at some point, WE have to do something about it if our "representatives" won't.

My point is that the harm occasioned by judicial activism--whether by liberal or conservative jurists--can be effectively thwarted IF IF IF the States and We the People assert their 9th and 10th Amendment constitutional powers.

Contrary to the opinion of many brainwashed law students, it is the U.S. Constitution--NOT the misleadingly named "Supreme" Court--which is the supreme law of the land, and both the 9th and 10th Amendments, both very much core components of that Constitution, were intended to safeguard *constitutional supremacy*, balance of powers and individual liberty.

When the delphic oracles of SCOTUS exceed their authority with unconstitutional rulings/opinions, then the States, per the 9th and the 10th Amendments, are legally and morally obliged to summarily nullify, aka render null, void and unenforceable, those rulings. In this regard, the framers' intention was crystal clear.

The Constitution works brilliantly to safeguard liberty, our core principles of checks and balances and separation of powers, but ONLY if it is honored and enforced by all parties to the federal-state contract we call the Constitution. And if the States, equal parties to that contract, are too weak-kneed or corrupted by federal handouts to honor the supreme law of the land, that being the Constitution and no other, then it is incumbent upon We the People, the final arbiters of what is and what is not constitutional, to assert our central role as the ultimate guardian of the Constitution. If that means well-coordinated nationwide civil disobedience and and other forms of defiance, then so be it! If it means patriots marching on and, yes, occupying our State houses to "convince" them to assert their authority over a runaway federal judiciary, so be it. No more pussy-footing, no more whining. Going forward, only meaningful a-c-t-i-o-n will suffice.

Let this sink in: only with the single-minded enforcement of the 9th and 10th Amendments by the States and/or the People can our constitutional republic be restored without resort to more assertive remedial actions. And the ball is clearly in OUR court!

In short, folks, we need to get very seriously organized. The growth of the imperial presidency, to say nothing of the Supreme Court's imperiousness, screams for remedial grassroots action.

In truth, the Supreme Court, a servant of the central government, has become an essentially unbridled, unaccountable, black-robed oligarchy, beholden to its federal overseers alone and driven by personal, political and ideological agendas. Tragically, the court's faithfulness to the Constitution has long ago dissipated. Revealingly, Gov. Hughes, who served as Chief Justice from 1930-1941, asserted that "We are under a Constitution, BUT the Constitution is what the judges say it is." Wow! And that pretty much sums up where we are now. Absent congressional remedial action, and without meaningful grassroots opposition, judicial supremacy will continue to effectively trump constitutional supremacy and, in so doing, the judiciary will continue to dangerously undermine the very underpinnings of our republic.

For me, THE burning question is this: by our disengagement, submissiveness, benign neglect, or by our merely hoping that the problem will eventually go away, will we continue to permit the foundational collapse of what little remains of our constitutional republic? We each need to honestly answer that question for ourselves and for our families.

("If the Federal Government should overpass the just bounds of its authority and make a tyrannical use of its powers, the PEOPLE, whose creature it is, must appeal to the standard they have formed [the Constitution], and take such measure to redress the injury to the Constitution as the exigency may suggest and prudence justify." Alexander Hamilton, Federalist Paper No. 33.)

("I know of no safe depository of the ultimate powers of the society but the people themselves; this is the true corrective of abuses of Constitutional powers." Thomas Jefferson)

(**"The great object of my fear is the federal judiciary. That body, like gravity, ever acting with noiseless foot and unlearning advance, gaining ground step by step and holding what it gains, is engulfing insidiously the state governments into the jaws of that which feeds them; the germ of dissolution of our federal government is in the constitution of the federal judiciary." Thomas Jefferson)**

A Powerful Judiciary is the Very Definition of Tyranny

For decades now, the Chief Executive, the Supreme Court and the mammoth unaccountable federal bureaucracy have been operating FAR FAR outside the Constitution, and too many folks just don't seem to get it or, worse, don't c-a-r-e.

By our silence and routine submission to this endless stream of lawlessness we, in effect, further weaken the Constitution and jeopardize those safeguards which it embodies.

The Chief Executive and the Judiciary MUST be reined in by Congress, failing which it is up to the States, per their 10th Amendment authority, to defy and nullify these non-stop encroachments on our liberty and the Rule of Law.

When it comes to the point that the strongest argument for supporting a GOP presidential candidate is to ensure that only "conservative" judges are appointed to fill court vacancies, shouldn't it then occur to us that by our merely asserting this argument exposes the awful truth that we have simply delegated far too much authority in the judiciary--FAR more authority than our Founders ever intended or could have ever envisioned.

When voters fear the appointment of either conservatives or liberals to the court, we are exposing our total ignorance of the constitutional role and limitations of the judiciary by our having accepted the wholly heretical notion that this judicial monster which now dominates our political system is the ultimate authority on legal, political and social issues. After all, don't these omniscient jurists obtain their infallible judgement and wisdom from God? Well, that is most certainly how most Americans view these black-robed oligarchs.

To checkmate judicial tyranny, the Constitution delegated to Congress the sacred duty to carefully vet federal judicial appointments to ensure that they are reliably committed to upholding the Rule of Law and the U.S. Constitution as originally ratified, failing which it is the constitutional duty of Congress to immediately impeach and remove any federal judge who violates that trust, be s/he Democrat or Republican, liberal or conservative.

In short, the proximate cause for the relentless stream of lawless, unconstitutional judicial rulings is FIRST, faithless, agenda-driven judges and SECOND, an unprincipled, spineless Congress unwilling to exercise its constitutional authority to impeach and remove demonstrably faithless judges.

The fault also lies with the States which routinely submit to judicial imperialism with but a faint whisper of objection. Per the 9th and 10th Amendments, States are absolutely empowered to render null and void any unconstitutional acts, not only of the federal court system, but also of the Chief Executive, the Congress and the fourth branch of government, the latter being that suffocating lawless federal bureaucracy which now routinely operates outside the Constitution.

So, why doesn't Congress impeach, and why do the States fail to protect their citizens from the blizzard of federal encroachments? In the case of our timid Congress, it is our reps' propensity for self-aggrandizement, ideological accommodation and political survival. In the case of the States, it is the mountains of federal hand-outs they receive for their submissiveness. In short, MONEY and POLITICAL SELF-INTEREST drive this government--not bedrock constitutional principles.

By original design, the States and Congress are the People's principal defenders of our rights to life, liberty and the pursuit of happiness. BUT it is the People who must ensure that our Founders' clear meaning and intentions are no longer ignored or flouted by local, State or federal apparatchiks. Thus, the ball is in our court. But, alas, what will we do with that ball? Kick it down the road again, or simply pretend it's not there.

As the ultimate arbiters of what is and is not constitutional, We, the creators of this federal constitutional republic, continue to ignore and dodge our responsibilities in this regard at our own peril.

Finally, I urge readers to join and support the Article V Convention of States whose sacred task it is to restore constitutional order, the ultimate guarantor of our Liberty. I also urge thoughtful readers to join and support the Tenth Amendment Center whose herculean efforts to restore the balance of power between States and the federal government has been nothing short of stellar.

("Seemingly guided by Chief Justice Hughes's arrogant and insidious assertion in 1941 that 'we are under a Constitution, but the Constitution is what the judges say it is', the court's unelected judicial oligarchs, aka judicial legislators, have, over the years, proven to be unreliable defenders of the Constitution." Author*)*

("The accumulation of all powers, legislative, executive, and judiciary, in the same hands, whether of one, a few, or many, and whether hereditary, self-appointed, or elective, may justly be pronounced the very definition of tyranny." James Madison, Federalist #47*)*

SCOTUS Must be Reined In

I tremble every time a serious constitutional question is put to the "Supreme Court".

Obvious to all but the willfully ignorant or ideologically blind, over the years SCOTUS has evolved into an essentially unbridled power unto itself. Guided by the principle of "judicial supremacy" vs "constitutional supremacy", and tainted by politics, ideology and a corrosive proclivity for social engineering, it has morphed into an unelected, unaccountable, black-robed judicial "Oligarchy of Nine", America's Politburo, whose constitutional moorings have long ago been essentially abandoned.

I can still recall the devastating words of Chief Justice Charles Evans Hughes in the 30's when he dropped all pretense of judicial faithfulness to the Constitution by haughtily proclaiming that *We are under a Constitution, but the Constitution is what the judges say it is.* Whoa, baby! Just let those insidious words sink in for a moment. Rather imperious, wouldn't you say? Just who deified these mere mortals? Most certainly NOT the founders. But thanks in part to an expansive *Marbury v Madison (1803)* ruling which vested exclusive authority in the Supreme Court for divining what is and what is not constitutional, the judicial tyranny has been on a judicial rampage ever since.

Clearly, we are seriously in need of a constitutional amendment to rein in our runaway courts, most particularly the Supreme Court. No less than Thomas Jefferson warned us against the encroaching, indeed despotic, power of the Supreme Court. Tragically, his warnings have been generally ignored, and we are now paying the awful price for having failed to properly and effectively challenge the reckless doctrine of "judicial supremacy".

That said, since SCOTUS has "ruled" in favor of Obamacare's individual mandate--or is it a tax?--should We the People yet again obediently submit because the Oligarchy of Nine ruled that we must? NOT ON YOUR LIFE--NOR MINE!!!!

Per the 9th and 10th Amendments, We the People and our immediate fiduciary agents, the States, must summarily nullify this repugnant ruling.

And that remedial action should be but the first step in a determined grassroots effort to rein in the runaway courts and the mortal jurists who populate them. Our founders and our progeny would expect nothing less of us.

As originally intended, We the People, the final arbiters and the "highest tribunal", are duty-bound to assert our constitutional authority when the "supreme court"--or any branch of the federal government--oversteps its original constitutional authority, failing which we deserve the cesspool of authoritarianism, social upheavel and economic ruin which will surely follow.

("There is no greater tyranny than that which is perpetrated under the shield of law and in the name of justice." Montesquieu*)*

Nullifying Judicial Overreach

Especially since 1895, the federal judiciary's role has shifted from that of ensuring "constitutional supremacy" to that of "judicial supremacy", surely a dangerous role shift which must be remedied.

Originally tasked with reviewing federal and state laws to ensure comportment with the Constitution, it has become disturbingly clear that the federal judiciary has dramatically strayed from its very limited constitutional role envisioned by the founders.

Without question, this foundational shift has dramatically altered the balance of power between the states and people on one side and the central government on the other, a carefully crafted balance which the framers had intended as a permanent and essential arrangement. As a result, the scope and power of the judiciary and, in turn, that of Congress and of the Executive Branch have profoundly expanded well beyond the limits intended by the framers.

In a letter to a friend in 1820, Thomas Jefferson asserted that "judicial review" had become a "dangerous doctrine", further warning that if unelected judges are permitted to be the "ultimate arbiters of all constitutional questions" at both the federal and state levels that a **"despotism of judicial oligarchy"** would surely ensue, resulting in the inevitable dissolution of the Republic. For me, that paragraph pretty much sums it up.

Even Alexander Hamilton, no faint-hearted proponent of a strong central government, warned that "the Courts must declare the sense of the law; and if they should be disposed to exercise WILL instead of JUDGMENT, the consequence would equally be the substitution of their pleasure to that of the legislative body."

He went on to counsel that **while an unconstitutional act of a legislature is null and void, so too is an unconstitutional act of the Supreme Court.** And since the Constitution is the creation of the people, he further asserted that **the Supreme Court must "measure all legislative acts against the will of the people" as set forth in the original Constitution.** So, it is clear that he viewed the court with a lingering sense of apprehension and doubt as well. Why?

Like Jefferson and his fellow founders, Hamilton well-understood the immutability of human nature and that man's proclivity for self-aggrandizement would always pose a threat to constitutional order. Thus, the framers intended that while the Supreme Court should be properly empowered to review legislative law, its strict fidelity to the original meaning and intent of the Constitution should always supersede all other obligations or personal biases. Obviously, a very tall order and, very likely, an unachievable goal for mere mortals. And so it has proven to be over the years.

The truth is that for all their perspicacity and diligence, the founders failed to fully and properly grasp the possibility of an overzealous judiciary. To wit, the only obvious checks imposed were as follows: 1) the appointment procedure involving both the President who nominates judges and the Senate which either consents to or disapproves those appointments; 2) Art III Sec 2 which empowers Congress to restrict the court's jurisdiction—which has rarely been attempted; 3) Congressional impeachment of judges for "treason, bribery, or other high crimes and misdemeanors", though the willful or erroneous interpretation of the original meaning of the Constitution was not considered grounds for removal--clearly, a yawning loophole. Precisely why this oversight was somehow permitted is, frankly, mystifying.

Strangely, the framers seem to have assumed that somehow these mortals, imbued with a fervent reverence for the Constitution, would steadfastly adhere to a strict interpretation of the Constitution in all their deliberations, stoically and nobly resisting political influences and selflessly ignoring their own social, ideological and economic predilections. Unsurprisingly, over the years this delusion on the part of the framers has resulted in a litany of gratuitous and arbitrary judicial opinions quite at odds with what Jefferson described as the *"honest meaning [of the Constitution] as contemplated by the people of the United States at the time of the [the Constitution's] adoption..."* In fact, in far too many instances, judicial opining has morphed into judicial legislating.

Firmly believing that the Constitution should at all times be strictly interpreted, Jefferson unambiguously counseled that *"on every occasion of construction, let us carry ourselves back to the time when the Constitution was adopted, recollect the spirit manifested in the debates, and instead of trying what meaning may be squeezed out of the text, or invented against it, conform to the probable one in which it was passed."* This approach is, of course, in direct conflict with the more contemporary concept of a "living and breathing Constitution" which, by its very nature, permits whimsical or otherwise subjective and transformational interpretations of the original Constitution by way of revisionist case law and agenda-driven rulings. With the discomforting specter of a living constitution evolving in the future, Jefferson admonished that *"our peculiar security is in the possession of a written Constitution. Let us not make it a blank paper by construction"* as our contemporary living constitution adherents have done so.

Compounding the seriousness of this matter, the absence of a Constitutionally-mandated standard of qualifications for judges was never included in the Constitution. As a result, history has shown that the judicial depth and constitutional motivations of many justices over the years have often been anything but stellar. This isn't to say that advanced law degrees alone should be the sole measure of a jurist's eligibility. Indeed, demonstrably unwavering faithfulness to original meaning and intent should determine one's eligibility to serve on the Supreme Court—or, for that matter, on any court, federal or state.

And where are we today?

Recall again these disturbing words of Gov. Hughes who served as Chief Justice from 1930 – 1941 during the heyday of the increasingly discredited New Deal: **"We are under a Constitution, but the Constitution is what the judges say it is."** Wowee! Thomas Jefferson's worst fears realized. And, yes, folks, that really is where we are today.

Clearly, the Supreme Court is out of control and has been in need of some serious reining in for some time now. As to a remedy, who better to consult on this matter than Mr. Jefferson himself who, in the early 19th century recommended the crafting of an amendment which would empower either Congress or the state legislatures (or both) to have veto and removal power over the Supreme Court. It was his view that the opinions of the Supreme Court should be subject to "some practical and impartial control," and that empowering a combination of federal and state authorities would accomplish that important goal.

However, we all know that a constitutional amendment process can be painfully deliberate, and, in the interim, much judicial mischief can be—and has been--inflicted on the country. So, what's the appropriate intervening solution to judicial overreach and error?

Very simply, nullification.

My advice is to urge State representatives and Attorneys General to prepare themselves and the citizens of their States for some honest to goodness push back of the 10th Amendment genre by letting the Supreme Court know that "we the people"—not the courts—are the final arbiters of what is and is not constitutional, My belief is that the threat of nullification alone may suffice to restrain judicial activism until a much needed and carefully crafted amendment is adopted.

In short, until an amendment is in place, all unconstitutional laws, rulings and executive orders must and ought to be subject to immediate State review and nullification. For example, since SCOTUS has gratuitously ruled against the States on Obamacare's "individual mandate', the States are now duty-bound to interpose—and should do so immediately and unhesitatingly.

For a start, a copy of this post was mailed to Atty Gen Cuccinelli of the great State of Virginia, the home and resting place of Thomas Jefferson.

But, this is only a start. All Attorneys General should be urged to encourage their States to nullify both the "individual mandate" as well as ANY unconstitutional laws/edicts/orders/rulings issued by DC in the future.

Tyranny on a Roll:
SCOTUS Again Subverts the Constitution

Looks like our invincibly arrogant Supreme Court is on a Progressive roll--a veritable steamroller of errant and overreaching Delphic rulings quite at odds with our Constitution.

On the heels of the Court's outrageous ruling yesterday on Obamacare, here it goes again by "ruling" that same-sex marriage is a "constitutional right". Huh? Constitutional right? This ruling is much more than mystifying; it is subversive.

While the same-sex ruling was entirely predictable--no less so than the Obamacare, aka SCOTUScare, ruling yesterday--I am no less stunned by this judicial quackery and lawlessness.

Thinking I may have missed something along the way, this morning I carefully re-read my copy of the Constitution, and for the life of me I couldn't find *marriage* of any kind defined as a "constitutional right". Nowhere! In fact, marriage isn't even mentioned in the text.

Per the 10th Amendment of the U.S. Constitution, any power not specifically/expressly delegated by the States to the federal government remains with the States and the People. Thus, defining marriage is a State power and same-sex marriage is constitutional ONLY if the individual State and its citizenry say it is. This isn't rocket science, folks. It's the law. And the obscene misapplication of the 14th Amendment's "equal protection" clause yet again cannot nullify the authority of the 9th and 10th Amendments. Only a constitutional amendment can do that.

Just what Constitution are these Progressive judicial oligarchs reading? Have they even read the Constitution? And, if so, do they at all regard the US Constitution as the supreme law of the land? Obviously not. Clearly, Judicial Supremacy has virtually supplanted Constitutional Supremacy. And therein lies the seed of our self-destruction.

Wouldn't it be splendid--indeed, principled and courageous--were the States to exercise their lawful authority by NULLIFYING this outrageous judicial usurpation of State sovereignty? Without spine and political courage at the State level, the US Constitution is, without question, D-E-A-D and this "constitutional republic" but an illusion.

Until this judicial tyranny is stopped, what precious remains of this tattered constitutional republic will be relegated to the dustbin of history.

I do not see a good end to this lawlessness. As to a remedy, let our Founders be our guide ...

("Today's decree says that my Ruler, and the Ruler of 320 million Americans coast-to-coast, is a majority of the nine lawyers on the Supreme Court. The opinion in these cases is the furthest extension in fact—and the furthest extension one can even imagine—of the Court's claimed power to create... liberties...that the Constitution and its Amendments neglect to mention. This practice of constitutional revision by an unelected committee of nine, always accompanied (as it is today) by extravagant praise of liberty, robs the People of the most important liberty they asserted in the Declaration of Independence and won in the Revolution of 1776: the freedom to govern themselves." **Justice Anthony Scalia**, June 26, 2015, regarding the same-sex SCOTUS ruling.*)*

States Yield Sovereign Authority to Federal Judiciary

To protest yet another round of invasive, heavy-handed "climate warming" regulations, fifteen States are suing the feds in FEDERAL court. Huh? Does anyone see something terribly flawed with that approach? Anyone?

WHY OH WHY OH WHY do States routinely appeal to the FEDERAL judiciary when a FEDERAL entity violates their sovereignty and constitutional authority? Why do States still cling to the self-destructive, delusional belief that the FEDERAL judicial oligarchy will somehow equitably defend State interests from FEDERAL excesses and lawlessness? WHY?

Think about it: if you had a property dispute with your neighbor, would you rely on your neighbor's attorney to represent your interests? Not if you have one operational brain cell left in your head!

EPA's latest round of draconian and unscientific "global warming" regulations is yet another clear case of FEDERAL overreach on steroids. If leaders in these States possessed even a modicum of principle and mettle, they would summarily invoke their 10th Amendment authority by NULLIFYING these damnably unconstitutional and unscientific EPA rulings. After all is said and done, a State's primary responsibility is to protect its citizens' liberty and well-being.

What the hell is wrong with these guys? Are they so accustomed to enslavement and federal hand-outs they are afraid to defend their sovereign interests from FEDERAL encroachment? Of course, that question is rhetorical. The unsettling truth is their needless obsequiousness has become habitual. (It appears that the awful effects of the so-called "civil war" which, among other things, reduced States to mere appendages of an unbridled central authority in DC, are still plaguing us.)

The short of it is that this spineless State reaction is symptomatic of a constitutional system in total foundational collapse. To believe we now live in a constitutional republic is utterly delusional.

What State dares to stand up to Leviathan and help restore constitutional? Who among us will finally stand up and stop this insanity and tyranny?!?!?!?!?

[8] CITIZENSHIP &
PRESIDENTIAL ELIGIBILITY

Natural-Born Citizenship: A Summary

Despite my 22 years of immigration counseling experience, trying to accurately and clearly summarize the issue of Obama's eligibility--or ineligibility--for the Presidency has been especially challenging and time-consuming. Though I have managed to compact much within this summary, I apologize in advance for the unavoidable length. Hope it proves to be a useful exercise.

CONTENTION: Obama was born in 1961 of a US Citizen mother and a British Citizen (born in Kenya); since Obama's father was not a US Citizen, thus not "attached to the US", Obama, even if born of a US Citizen mother within the jurisdiction of the US, is not, by definition and Constitutional intent, a "natural born citizen" as is specifically required by Article II, Sec 1 (Presidential Clause) of the US Constitution, and is, therefore, ineligible to assume the Office of the President.

British citizenship was conferred to Obama at birth by act of British law. Thus, he was born of dual citizenship.

Art II, Sec 1 of the Constitution, the so-called Presidential Clause, stipulates that *"No Person except a* **natural born Citizen**, *or a Citizen of the United States at the time of the Adoption of this Constitution, shall be eligible to the Office of the President; neither shall any Person be eligible to* *that Office who shall not have attained the Age of thirty five Years, and been fourteen Years a Resident within the United States."*

Within the context of the Framers' actual meaning (letter of the law) and the Framers' express purpose (intent), being a "natural born citizen" requires that citizenship must be passed on by the constitutionally pertinent principle of natural law (see *Law of Nations* by E. Vatel-1758 which profoundly influenced the Framers' intent when fashioning the Constitution) and which assumes that *citizenship is inherited from one's father's citizenship.* To wit, Vatel stated that "natives", or *natural-born citizens, are those born in the country of parents who are citizens"*, and that "as society cannot exist and perpetuate itself otherwise than by the children of the citizens, *those children naturally follow the condition of their fathers,* and succeed to all their right." <u>Again, the accent is on the father's citizenship status at the time of the child's birth.</u>

The intent of the Framers with respect to the meaning of "natural born citizen" (vs "born in the US" or "US Citizen") within the context of the Presidential Clause specifically takes into account the *father's allegiance and citizenship at the time of a child's birth.* Thus, the father's citizenship and, thus, his "attachment to the US" at the time of the child's birth, carried more weight than merely the geographic location of the child's birth. Why? Still reeling from British rule, the Framers, as represented by the words of John Jay in a July 1787 letter to George Washington, the latter who presided over the Constitutional Convention, wanted to avoid dual citizenship or dual loyalties of any future Commander-in-Chief by declaring expressly "that the Commander-in-Chief...shall not be given to nor devolve on, any but a **natural born citizen"**, this to insure future leadership's freedom from foreign influences.

This correspondence directly influenced how Art II, Sec 1 was subsequently written, which holds that "no person except a natural born citizen, or a citizen of the United States at the time of the Adoption of the Constitution, shall be eligible to the Office of the President." (Notice the distinction. By definition, the Founders couldn't possibly be natural born citizens and necessarily exempted themselves from that requirement.)

The first <u>Nationality Act in 1790</u> declared that "the children of citizens [plural] of the United States, that may be born beyond the sea, or out of the limits of the United States, shall be considered as natural born citizens: Provided, That *the right of citizenship shall not descend to persons whose fathers have never been resident in the United States."* (Notice what appeared to be the central importance of the father's status.)

However, the <u>Naturalization Act of 1795</u> stated that children born to citizens beyond the seas are "citizens" of the United States but are not "natural born citizens" of the United States. (A more exclusionary definition which adds the geographic requirement as well.)

Also, we should note that the primary author of the citizenship clause in the 14th Amendment, Sen. Jacob Howard, declared that the citizenship clause of the Amendment was, again, by virtue of "natural law" and not by "act of law" (statute). This would mean that a child born to a US Citizen father was "natural born".

In 1871, Rep. John Bingham, a Framer of the 14th Amendment, stated that a child is a US Citizen if born of naturalized parents inasmuch as a naturalized father as part of the naturalization oath "absolutely renounces and abjure all allegiance and fidelity" to other sovereignties, thus establishing his firm "attachment to the United States" as well. (So, *born of US Citizen parents within the jurisdiction* are the overriding factors in determining "natural born citizenship.")

Note too that US Title 8 Sec 1401 provides that US Citizenship alone is not sufficient to qualify one for President or Vice President, the clear inference being that he or she must be natural born.

In 1800, Charles Pinkney, a Framer of the Constitution and, later, the S.C. Governor, said that the Presidential Clause was designed to firmly "insure attachment to the country." (No dual loyalties on the part of either parent.)

Art IV, Sec 2 provided that no act of Congress was required to make citizens of the individual states citizens of the US; only State Legislatures had authority to grant State citizenship which, in turn, conferred upon them US Citizenship.

Further, in <u>*Savage vs Umphries (TX) 118 S.W. 893, 909*</u>, the court ruled that *"as a man is a citizen of the country to which his father owes allegiance,* it is incumbent on one alleging in an election contest that a voter is not a citizen of the US to show that such voter's father was not a citizen thereof during his son's minority."

In 1820, Rep. A. Smith (VA), stated that "when we apply the term citizens to the inhabitants of States, it means those who are members of the political community. *The civil law determined the condition of the son by that of the father.* A man whose father was not a citizen was allowed to be a perpetual inhabitant, but not a citizen, unless citizenship was conferred on him."

And what does the 14th Amendment have to say about this?

The primary author of the citizenship clause in the 14th, Sen. Jacob Howard, declared that the citizenship clause of the Amendment was, again, by virtue of "natural law" and not by "act of law". This would mean that a child born to a US Citizen father is, therefore, "natural born".

In 1866, per the 14th Amendment, the terms "subject to the jurisdiction of the US" was defined as meaning "not owing allegiance to any other sovereignty." In the same year, Sec 1992 of US Revised Statutes declared that "all persons born in the US and not subject to any foreign power, excluding Indians not taxed, are declared to be citizens of the US."

In 1871, Rep. John Bingham, a framer of the 14th, stated that a child is a US Citizen if born of naturalized parents inasmuch as a naturalized father as part of the naturalization oath "absolutely renounces and abjures all allegiance and fidelity" to other sovereignties, thus establishing his firm "attachment to the United States" as well. So, it would seem that born of US Citizen parents within the jurisdiction of the US are the overriding and defining factors in determining "natural born citizenship".

In Sec. 1992, Rep. John Bingham, stated that "every human being born within the jurisdiction of the US of parents [plural] not owing allegiance to any foreign sovereignty is, in the language of the Constitution itself, a natural born citizen." (Very definitive for purposes both of the 14th Amendment and the Presidential Clause.)

*See _Perkins vs ELG, US 325 (1939)_ ruling which provides <u>the two criteria</u> <u>expressed by Rep. John Bingham must exist before one can be called a</u> <u>"natural born citizen."</u>

On June 22, 1874, Congress issued a joint resolution that stated the "United States has not recognized a double allegiance."

Of contemporaneous interest is that according to the US State Department's Foreign Affairs Manual (7 FAM 1131.6-2 Eligibility for Presidency), "the fact that someone is a natural born citizen pursuant to a statute ["natural born citizen" and "by statute" are incongruous) does not necessarily imply that he or she is such a citizen for Constitutional purposes." The incongruity created by the statement's use of "natural born citizen" and "by statute" notwithstanding, it appears that a naturalized citizen (by law/statute) is not eligible to assume the office of the President, but it seems to be generally agreed that children born within the jurisdiction of the US of naturalized parents are considered to be "natural born citizens" since that child's parents are, as part of the naturalization process, required "to renounce and abjure any allegiance or fidelity to any foreign sovereignty" and, thus, are, at the time of the child's birth, "attached to the US." Similarly, and more obviously, a child born within US jurisdiction of two US citizen parents is also considered a "natural born citizen".

So, it appears that there is no better way to insure "attachment to the US" then to require the President to have inherited his American citizenship from his US Citizen father or from both his US citizen parents. The Framers' rationale for this would be that any child born in the US of an alien father, or a father of dual allegiance, can be removed by their father to be reared in another country only to be returned later in life bringing with him/her foreign influences. Thus, for purposes of complying with the Presidential Clause, a person born of dual citizenship/allegiance cannot be said to be a natural born citizen. Again, and within the context of the Presidential Clause, the child inherits natural born citizenship from the father alone because, through the laws of nature, the child inherits the condition of the father.

Within the meaning of the Presidential Clause, one can accurately say that there are essentially two types of citizenship: 1) "natural born citizenship" meaning one who, by operation of nature (descent), was born of an American citizen father, or, as further expanded upon in successive legislation and opinion, was born of two US Citizen parents, and 2) a "US Citizen" meaning one who, through operation of law (statutory) was granted citizenship through naturalization, either automatically at time of birth or voluntarily sometime after birth. (See John Bingham opinion above.)

The recent *Wrotnowski vs Bysiewica* stay request which was denied by SCOTUS on 12/15/08 asserts that Pres. Chester A. Arthur's father was a British citizen at the time of Chester's birth--and the facts appear to clearly substantiate that assertion--and that, therefore, Chester A. Arthur was ineligible under Art II, Sec 1 to assume the office of President. And since the facts of the Arthur case were very similar to that of Obama's, it was plaintiff's hope to force the Court to review Obama's eligibility to be President as well.

In *Happersett vs Minor (1875)*, this: "The Constitution does not in words say who shall be natural-born citizens. Resort must be had elsewhere to ascertain that. At common law, with the nomenclature of which the framers of the Constitution were familiar, it was never doubted that all children born in a country of parents who were its citizens became themselves, upon their birth, citizens also. These were natives or *natural-born citizens*, as distinguished from aliens or foreigners."

So, even if Obama verifies his birth within the jurisdiction of the US, he is a US Citizen by virtue of his mother's American citizenship, but he is not a natural born citizen because he was born of an alien father and is, therefore, not, by definition and intent of the Presidential Clause, a natural born citizen.

And if Pres. Chester A. Arthur was ineligible to be President because his father was a British citizen at the time of Chester's birth, should the Supreme Court rule Chester Arthur's breach of law a defensible precedent for granting Presidential eligibility to Obama since his father too was a British citizen at the time of Obama's birth in 1961? On this question, the Framers' method for repairing the breach is per constitutional amendment. Clearly, the Framers did not want a President at birth to be born of dual citizenship. As someone much smarter than I said, "making errors in the past does not mean that we need to repeat them in the future."

**From this summary of law, I think it can be *most reasonably*
concluded that since a child derives his attachment to the US from
his US Citizen parents, a child born of US Citizen parents within
the jurisdiction of the US, inclusive of those US parents who were
naturalized US citizens at the time of the child's birth, is very clearly
a "natural born citizen".**

Finally, this from Thomas Jefferson in a letter to Judge Wm. Johnson in
1823: "On every question of construction of the Constitution, let us carry
ourselves back to the time when the Constitution was adopted, recollect
the spirit manifested in the debates, and instead of trying what meaning
may be squeezed out of the text, or intended against it, conform to the
probably intent in which it was passed."

And this from Pres. George Washington in his Farewell Address in 1796:
"If, in the opinion of the people, the distribution or modification of the
constitutional powers be in any particular way wrong, let it be corrected by
an amendment in the way which the Constitution designates. But let there
be no change by usurpation; for through this, in one instance, may be the
instrument of good, it is the customary weapon by which free governments
are destroyed."

Absent the Electors' having denied Certification of the Election or
individual lawmakers demanding verification of Obama's eligibility,
it is properly left to SCOTUS, Congress or the amendment process to
determine the constitutional eligibility of Obama to assume the Office
of the President. Allowing this constitutional issue to fester could have
unintended and very unsettling consequences for our country in the
future. If the Constitution is to be ignored or conveniently misinterpreted,
the Rule of Law will suffer yet another setback.

Until this issue is authoritatively and constitutionally resolved, we have a
problem. A real problem.

Birthright Citizenship & Judicial Incompetence (8/2015)

Mindful of the litany of revisionist case law since the Constitution's ratification, it is clear that *stare decisis* is a judicial principle fraught with constitutional perils. Why? One corrupted court ruling inevitably leads to another, compounding the corruption of original intent merely for the shortsighted and self-serving purpose of sanctifying precedent—a surefire judicial recipe for eventually ruling the Constitution out of existence.

In this regard, Thomas Jefferson was right when he viewed with horror the growing menace of a runaway Supreme Court which increasingly valued "judicial supremacy" and personal agendas over "constitutional supremacy".

And so it is with the libertine and gratuitous 1898 ruling in *US v Wong Kim Ark*.

On the issue of birthright citizenship, liberals breathlessly invoke this precedent-setting and fundamentally flawed ruling to justify their *feeling* that children born on US soil (*jus soli*) of illegal immigrants are and ought to be automatically entitled to US Citizenship. Wow! How very humanitarian, but how terribly misguided.

First off, let me point out that amending the constitution in order to deny automatic citizenship to children of illegal aliens is totally unnecessary. Since the 14th Amendment already very clearly stipulates that children of aliens cannot be legally granted US citizenship on the basis of birthplace alone (*jus soli*), perhaps, at most, a congressional act or a trenchant SCOTUS ruling is all that is needed, this to merely re-clarify and restate what the 14th Amendment already says and, more importantly, to expunge from our jurisprudential history this embarrassingly irresponsible Wong Kim Ark ruling once and for all.

As said, the inescapable result of judicially ignoring original intent and meaning is to pile corrupted case law atop corrupted case law. To wit, in *Plyler v Doe* (1967), SCOTUS, relying on the revisionist Wong Kim Ark opinion and failing to consult the actual meaning of the 14th's "subject to the jurisdiction thereof" wording, ruled that children of illegal aliens who simply reside in a state may be considered to be within the jurisdiction of the US. In effect, Wong Kim Ark and Plyler simply and imperiously ignored original meaning, thus violating their sacred oath to uphold the Constitution. If nothing else, these rulings readily attest to the inherent corruptibility and unreliability of self-deified jurists.

When fervently invoking Wong Kim Ark, what the birthright adherents fail to tell you—probably because many of them are either honestly ignorant or willfully dismissive of the facts—is that this ruling, made out of whole cloth, arrogantly, incompetently and unceremoniously contradicted *Elk v Wilkins* (1884) which, in keeping with the 14th, ruled that birthplace alone (*jus soli*) was insufficient grounds to grant US Citizenship.

The contrived Wong Kim Ark ruling also ignored the earlier Supreme Court discussion of the 14th Amendment in the *Slaughterhouse* cases wherein the court noted that *"the phrase 'subject to the jurisdiction thereof' was intended to exclude ...children of ministers, consuls, and citizens and subjects of foreign States born within the United States."*

Clearly, the Wong Kim Ark majority didn't allow facts to get in their way. Like liberals today, they follow precedent ONLY when it suits their predispositions and political agendas.

Some may recall that the 14th's framers were painstakingly specific about the meaning of "subject to the jurisdiction thereof". A quick review of those particular quotes which so many on the left have either deliberately ignored or overlooked clearly shows-- irrefutably--that, unlike the majority opinion in this case, the 14th's framers understood that "subject to the jurisdiction thereof" was synonymous with "not owing allegiance to any foreign power". The inescapable point: you cannot be subject to the jurisdiction of the United States if you are legally subject to the jurisdiction of a foreign power. Duh. But, very briefly, here again is what the 14th's framers actually said.

Framer Sen. Trumbell noted that the goal of this statute was *"to make citizens of everybody born in the US who owe allegiance to the US."* He went on to explain that *"all persons born in the US, and subject to the jurisdiction thereof, are citizens; this means subject to the complete jurisdiction thereof. And what do we mean by 'complete jurisdiction thereof'? Not owing allegiance to anybody else. That is what it means."*

Sen. Trumbell didn't mince words. He didn't say temporarily or partially within US jurisdiction, but <u>completely</u> within US jurisdiction. With that explanation from a principal framer of the 14th, how then can the most ardent birthright citizenship advocate reasonably and clear-headedly trumpet the merits and judicial reliability of Wong Kim Ark? In truth, the objective and honest among them can't without at least a little embarrassment. But, sadly, that won't stop them from mindlessly railing against birthright citizenship opponents anyway. It's what they do.

Concurring with Trumbell, Sen. Jacob Howard asserted that *"the word 'jurisdiction' as here employed, ought to be construed so as to imply a <u>full and complete jurisdiction</u> on the part of the US, coextensive in all respects with the constitutional power of the US, whether exercised by Congress, the executive, or by the judicial department; that is to say, the same jurisdiction in extent and quality as applies to every citizen of the US."* Obviously, he wasn't talking about a temporary visitor or illegal entrant with foreign ties.

In 1866, Cong. James Wilson of the House Judiciary Committee asserted *"we must depend on the general law relating to subjects and citizens recognized by all nations for a definition, and that must lead us to the conclusion that every person born in the United States is a natural-born citizen of such States, <u>except that of children born on our soil to temporary sojourners</u> or representatives of a foreign government."*

Framer John Bingham said that this statute meant *"every human being born within the jurisdiction of the United States of parents not owing allegiance to any foreign sovereignty is, in the language of the Constitution itself, a* **natural-born citizen.***"* (Finally, a definition of "natural-born citizen".) Clearly, then, the jurisdictional status of the child's parents (*jus sanguinis*) was every bit as important as the birthplace of the child in determining a child's citizenship. Thus, US citizenship is predicated BOTH on birthplace (*jus soli*) and parentage (*jus sanguinis*). Of course, that's clear, but the agenda-driven left just doesn't want to hear of it.

It's also important to note that **Sec 1992 of US Revised Statutes**, the same Congress which adopted the 14th Amendment confirmed that "all persons born in the United States <u>and not subject to any foreign power</u>... are declared to be citizens of the United States."

And this thought: if one's allegiance to the US can be properly determined by birth alone in the US (*jus soli*), then why do we require legal immigrants to renounce their allegiance to their motherlands for purposes of naturalization? In short, folks, the Wong Kim Ark ruling is not only baffling, it makes absolutely no sense at all!

Also, in the Wong Kim Ark ruling, legally indefensible though it is, shouldn't it be of more than passing interest to note some mysterious wording in that ruling as well?

The ruling: "A child born in the United States, of parent[s] of Chinese descent, who, at the time of his birth, <u>are subjects of the Emperor of China</u>, but have a permanent domicile and residence in the United States, and are there carrying on business, and are not employed in any diplomatic or official capacity under the Emperor of China, becomes at the time of his birth a citizen of the United States."

Huh? The parents are subjects of the Emperor of China, yet because they are domiciled and carrying out business in the USA their child is magically eligible for US citizenship? By what twist of logic do those conditions confer US citizenship on the child? Just asking.

Frankly, despite a rather exhaustive search I can find no scholarly explanation for this conspicuously incoherent ruling. <u>Upon what previous ruling did the court draw those words? Certainly not from the 14th's framers, and most certainly not from the Constitution's founders!</u> That alone should give our erudite lefty friends at least a modicum of intellectual pause. But, probably not. They apply the law to fit their agendas, and casually ignore that which doesn't advance their political game plan. Heaven forbid should they stoop to seeking original constitutional intent and meaning. Horrors!

Another point: the court's majority justified their ruling on the basis of English common law. What?!?!? US citizenship law had broken with English common law tradition after independence (which included the tortured English doctrine of "perpetual allegiance" over which America clashed with Britain in the War of 1812). Sen. Howard clearly explained that the citizenship clause was based upon "natural law and national law", never in any way alluding to English common law. (Note: from all I have read, E. Vattel's concept of a child inheriting his/her father's citizenship by descent (*jus sanguinis*), regardless of birthplace, manifestly dominated US legal history after independence, and it was E. Vattel's <u>Law of Nations</u> which so profoundly influenced our founders and the 14th's framers.)

Also, if anyone takes the time to read the dissenting opinions in this grotesque ruling, one would be regaled with thoughtful and scholarly constitutional opinion. But, that's not what the left wants. It wants a solid and burgeoning voter bloc, this to keep their sorry lot in power. But, I do have to ask what possessed the majority in Wong Kim Ark to rule as they did. It certainly wasn't their strong sense of fidelity to the Constitution. Unbridled compassion or snuff?

So, in summary, the legality of birthright citizenship is a breathtakingly obvious hoax perpetrated by judicial revisionists and encouraged by stridently vocal ideologically-driven birthright citizenship adherents. At this point, all we can reasonably hope for is a sober and timely SCOTUS review which, God-willing, will do the unthinkable, that being actually upholding the rule of law. Sure hope that's not too much to ask. But, I'm not holding my breath...

("A refusal to consider reliable evidence of original intent in the Constitution is no more excusable than a judge's refusal to consider legislative intent." Justice John Paul Stevens re the Wong Kim Ark ruling.*)*

[9] THE GLOBAL
WARMING HUSTLE

The Odious Global Warming Deception

Smugly impervious to scientific reasoning and appeals for open scientific debate, an international cabal of histrionic socialist ideologues, authoritarians, politicians and academicians in league with a greedy rabble of financial opportunists and sell-outs in the science community continue to shamelessly assert that menacing man-made global warming is a done deal, that there is a "scientific consensus" on that score, and that the growing number of respected scientific critics are but terribly misguided "crackpots", "Neanderthals", and heretical "flat earthers".

Absent unassailable scientific data to support their claims of cataclysmic global warming, and with mounting objective evidence of fraudulent manipulation of that data, in archetypal Leftist fashion the elitist global warming gang has resorted to the usual mindless torrent of tedious ad hominem to both intimidate scientific critics and to altogether shut down scientific debate. How very reassuring.

Predictably, capricious Leftist ideology is again trumping commonsense, rationality and responsible stewardship. And, once again, "we the people", meticulously disdained by our patrician overseers here and abroad, are expected to compliantly pick up the lavish and painful costs of their spectacular folly.

Thus, their cynical goal remains the same: the fundamental transformation of the Western World into a wonderland of mediocrity, enforced equality and diminished standards of living--but, of course, with these illustrious intellectual giants in charge of every facet of our worthless plebeian lives.

In a nutshell, isn't this precisely what it's really all about? When will this madness stop?

Positively mind-boggling!

Beware Environmentalist Tyranny (06/2008)

Al Gore's oft-repeated assertion there exists a "consensus" within the scientific community that human activity has accelerated global warming to perilous levels was officially and strongly rejected last month by thousands of participating scientists of the Oregon Institute of Science & Medicine (OISM).

Debunking the climatic doomsday scenarios advanced by Gore, environmental activists and their opportunistic political allies in D.C., 31,000 scientists petitioned the U.S. Government to reject Kyoto or any similar proposals noting that dire "predictions of harmful climatic effects due to future increases in minor greenhouse gases like CO2 are in error and do not conform to current experimental knowledge" and that "proposed limits on greenhouse gases would [in fact] harm the environment, hinder the advance of science and technology, and damage the health and welfare of mankind."

With scientific certitude, their petition maintained that "there is no convincing scientific evidence that human release of CO2, methane or other greenhouse gases is causing, or will in the foreseeable future cause, catastrophic heating of the Earth's atmosphere and disruption of Earth's climate."

The petition went on to state that "there is substantial evidence that increased CO2 is environmentally helpful...creating many beneficial effects upon the natural plant and animal environments of the Earth."

It should be noted that the countervailing "scientific consensus" about which Gore and his minions are so fond of citing reflects the viewpoints of 600 scientists who represent less than 1% of the worldwide scientific community! Do the math. So much for "consensus", huh?

Is it any wonder why Gore stubbornly and nimbly refuses to openly debate the "issue" with those representing a divergent *scientific* view?

Ah, yet again, another shattered myth perpetuated by our ambitious friends on the far left. Looks like the high priests of environmentalism will soon need to find another way to advance their dreams of social control and political dominance. We can only hope that their fall from grace occurs before they've managed to completely wreck our and the world's economy.

("The largest threat to freedom, democracy, the market economy, and prosperity is no longer socialism. It is, instead, the ambitious, arrogant, unscrupulous ideology of environmentalism." Pres. Vaclav Klaus, President of Czech Republic, May '08)

Global Warming or Global Cooling (09/2008)

Though difficult, one can still cull authoritative information which scientifically contests politically correct viewpoints regarding global warming. And with costly global warming-friendly legislation such as cap-and-trade threatening us all, we should do our best to stay informed.

In my June 9th post, I reported on the May 2008 submission of a petition to Congress and the President by 31,000 scientists representing the Oregon Institute of Science & Medicine which debunked doomsday global warming scenarios (such as those advanced by Gore and his political allies) and which warned against ill-conceived legislative fixes.

Now these latest tidbits from the scientific community:

1. Canadian climatologist T. Ball warns that "if we are facing a [global climate] crisis at all, it is that we are preparing for warming when we should be preparing for cooling."

2. Australian scientist Peter Harris asserts that "the Earth is nearing the end of the typical interglacial cycle and is due for a sudden cooling climate change." He goes on to say that "based upon careful analysis we can say that there is a 94% probability of imminent global cooling and the beginning of the coming ice age." He notes that climate is currently unstable and that "most of the natural climate processes we are witnessing now are interdependent and occur at the end of each interglacial period, ultimately causing sudden long-term cooling."

3. Noting that over the last 500,000 years there is a **100%** correlation between gravitational cycles to the beginning and ending of global warming cycles, in his book, **Global Warming - Global Cooling, Natural Causes Found**, the culmination of 19 years of research, meteorologist D. Dilley writes that "by 2023 global climate temperatures will become similar to colder temperatures in the 1800's."

4. The Russian Academy of Sciences warns that "Earth is now at the peak of one of its passing warm spells which started in the 17th century when there was no industrial influence on the climate and no such thing as the hothouse effect." In a companion story, Oleg Sorakan

of the Academy notes that "carbon dioxide is not to blame for global change," and goes on to say that "solar activity is many times more powerful than the energy produced by the whole of humankind."

5. Victor Herrera, a Mexican geophysicist, reports that global warming prognostications "are incorrect because they are based solely upon mathematical models and present results from scenarios that do not include solar activity." He concludes that "in 2 years or so there will be the beginnings of a little ice age that will last 60-80 years" and that "the immediate consequences of this will be drought."

6. UK astrophysicist P. Corbyn asserts that "there is no evidence that CO2 has ever driven or ever will drive world temperatures and climate change. Worrying about CO2 is irrelevant." And where have we heard that before?

7. A recent U.S. Senate committee report highlighted Russian physicists' collective projection that "global temperatures will cool--not warm--within the next decade."

So, despite the politicization of the subject, and the beltway's general acceptance of global warming as an incontrovertible fact of life, what is actually occurring in our global climate is still hotly contested among rank and file scientists.

On such a weighty subject, transparent and responsible **scientific** discussion of the subject at the national level should be demanded. A "climate change commission" comprised of scientists--not political hacks--who represent a variety of scientific viewpoints and perspectives on the subject of climate change should be immediately convened to develop a coherent body of data and recommendations for the consideration of both Congress and the President. Our government's attempting to legislate without the benefit of intelligent, apolitical scientific discussion is both shortsighted and insane. The damage to the country caused by the lethal mix of politics with science could be incalculable.

Climate Warming Myth Exposed (12/2008)

Dare attack the Eco-Movement high priests, and you may find yourself out in the cold.

Enter Dr. Will Happer: A Princeton University physicist and a fellow of the American Physical Society and the Nat'l Academy of Sciences, Dr. Happer had been Dir. of Energy Research (1990-1993) during the Clinton Administration until fired by Al Gore for "refusing to go along with Gore's alarmism" about global warming. Dr. Happer asserts that **"he had been told in 1993 that science was not going to intrude on policy."** He went on to point out that "fears about man-made global warming are unwarranted and are not based on good science. The earth's climate is changing now, as it always has, and that there is *no evidence* that the changes differ in any qualitative way from those of the past."

Continuing to scan a plethora of climate warming-related articles, it has become more than obvious that the man-made climate change myth is driven by ideological and political agendas, greed and power. Absolutely nothing more.

Blithely ballyhooed by the media, the man-made climate change mythology has been perpetrated by the effete liberal elites and their willing political cohorts in Washington. The short of it is that the "climate warming movement", a religious movement in its own right, is probably every bit as dangerous to the modern world as is Islamofascism, both being clear and present dangers to our liberty and our very way of life.

Dr. Happer joins a large number of respected scientists who are courageously countering the global warming hoax, and their ranks are growing exponentially. And while climate warming elites in America embark on what could be a sweeping and costly program to counter man-made global warming, Europe, a hotbed of socialist drivel, is already backing off Kyoto and the economically debilitating cap-and-trade program. Will America learn from Europe's mistakes? Right now, I'd say it's a better than even chance it won't. To paraphrase George Will, "The one surefire lesson of history is that we don't ever seem to learn from it."

Not surprisingly, dissenting scientists around the world have been scorned, shunned and their livelihoods threatened for their apostasy. These folks are owed an immense debt of gratitude for bucking the alarmist tide and for courageously speaking up against global warming true-believers.

In addition to the 31,000 scientists from the Oregon Institute of Science & Medicine whose urgent petition to both the White House and Congress in May 2008 stated that "there is **no convincing scientific evidence** that human release of CO2, methane and other greenhouse gases is causing, or will in the foreseeable future, cause, catastrophic heating of the Earth's atmosphere and disruption of Earth's climate," in 2007 and 2008 over 650 additional climatologists and other reputable scientists around the world have similarly and openly debunked the myth. Among them, these notables as well:

1. Ivar Giaever, Nobel Prize Winner for Physics: "I am a skeptic. **Global warming has become a new religion.**"

2. Dr. Joanne Simpson, Atmospheric Scientist, formerly of NASA: "**Since I am no longer receiving funding, I can speak frankly...**As a scientist I remain skeptical of global warming."

3. Dr. Kiminori Itoh, Environmental Physical Chemist: "**When people come to know what the truth is, they will feel deceived by science and scientists.**"

4. Dr. David Gee, Geologist, Uppsala University of Sweden: "For how many years must the planet cool before we begin to understand that the planet is not warming."

5. James A. Peden, Atmospheric Physicist: "**Many scientists are now searching for a way to back out quietly (from promoting climate warming fears), without having their professional careers ruined.**"

6. Prof. Delgado Domingos, Environmental Scientist: **Creating an ideology pegged to carbon dioxide is dangerous nonsense. The present alarm on climate change is an instrument of social control.**"

7. Dr. Takeda Kunihiko, Vice-Chancellor, Institute of Science
    &Technology, Chubu University: **"Every scientist knows that CO2
    emissions make absolutely no difference one way or another, but
    it doesn't pay to say so."**

8. Dr. Bruce West, US Army Chief Scientist: ***"Sun, not man, is driving
    climate change."***

9. Dr. David Deming, Geophysicist & Assoc. Prof. Arts & Sciences,
    Univ. of Oklahoma: "It is time to file this theory (global warming) in
    the ashbin of history. Alarmists are in denial and running for cover."

10. Dr. E. Wegman, Nat'l Academy of Sciences, Prof. H. Tenehes, Royal
    Netherlands Meteorological Institute, Dr. A. Zichini, renowned
    Physicist, Dr. Z. Jaworowski, world expert on ancient ice cores, Prof.
    T.V. Segalstad, University of Oslo's Geological Museum, Dr. Claude
    Allegre, US Nat'l Academy of Sciences, have all joined in "rejecting
    **global warming theory as scientifically unsound, implausible,
    fraudulent."**

And these tidbits from scientific studies:

1. Europe's cap-and-trade program has been a disaster, yet the Obama
    Administration remains enamored of Kyoto and cap-and-trade. Duh...

2. Since the release of High Priest Gore's "Inconvenient Truth", the
    earth's temp has dropped by 1/3 degree Celsius.

3. If the US reduces carbon emissions by 75% by 2050, it would result in
    just .013 degree Celcius of "prevented" warming by 2050.

4. Without the participation of India and China, even if the U.S, Europe
    & Japan were to take every vehicle off the road and shut off every
    power plant, atmospheric CO2 would still climb from the current 35
    parts per million to 450 ppm by 2070.

5. Had the Lieberman-Warner cap-and-trade plan been implemented,
    economists determined it would have cost the US economy $4-8
    trillion in GNP and a net loss of 1 million jobs by 2030.

I thought Doug Giles of Townhall.com nicely summed it up this way: **"The specious science of global warming establishes truth not by facts but through NON-STOP REPETITION."** (Now, where have we seen that familiar strategy before?) He goes on to say that "everything is being blamed on global warming from summer frost in Africa, snow storms in Las Vegas, freezing penguin chicks, poorly rising bread dough, terrorism, forest fires in California, hurricanes, impoverished fashion houses and the recent economic downturn suffered by whorehouses in Belgium." Amazing. More to the point, INSANE!

Could anything be plainer: on the matter of global warming, there is NO scientific consensus. Zilch. Zero. Nada. Thus, before our leadership commits our fast-dwindling fortunes to attacking windmills, shouldn't the entire subject be openly, honestly and objectively discussed by a Commission of respected SCIENTISTS representing all points of view on the subject? Only then should we contemplate draconian spending programs to reduce our so-called "carbon footprint." Is that really too much to ask? Unfortunately for us all, in these politically correct times of "governing by sound bites & repetition" I suspect many hardened Leftists will continue to blindly follow like sheep to slaughter..........

Climate Warming Myth Nails
US Taxpayers Again (01/2009)

Citing the specter of ruinous man-made global warming and national security considerations as his rationale, BHO ordered an already bankrupt car industry to accelerate the development and marketing of "green cars" by 2011 (9 years earlier than the original goal) and to allow a patchwork of states to unilaterally impose more stringent emissions standards which will further aggravate already seriously declining auto sales. How that's going to create jobs or rescue the auto industry is beyond me.

Already dependent upon taxpayer bailouts to stay afloat, the auto industry estimates the cost of compliance with this incredibly foolish executive order to run as high as $100 billion! And guess who's going to foot the bill for that insanity? The already besieged taxpayers, of course. But, to the New Order, any reasoned dissent or unpleasant truth is a "distraction", an oft-used Obamaism connoting unworthiness of attention or consideration. So, get used to the bailouts and condescension, my taxpaying comrades.

While ensuring that our country is not held hostage by foreign energy producers is a worthy goal, this isn't the way to do it. Clearly, holding the auto industry and taxpayers hostage is not a sensible solution to our energy problems. Getting a comprehensive energy plan off the ground is.

BHO's edict accomplishes nothing more than placating the enviro-extremist lobbyists and their opportunistic climate warming disciples on Capitol Hill. Does it help the country? NO! Will it produce more jobs? NO! Will it work? Well, if the bailouts are gargantuan enough, then just maybe. But, to what end? To advance a shortsighted, asinine ideology and nothing more.

As our tendentiously liberal Democrat &Chronicle newspaper loftily stated, BHO's intention is to ensure that "science will trump ideology and special interests..." Surely, another mindless progressive moment for the paper. Just who's kidding whom? Following raucous laughter, my bet is that the over 4,000 eminent and increasingly vocal scientists around the world who have publicly voiced their *scientific* opposition to the man-made global warming fabrication would take umbrage at the D&C's baseless UNscientific assertion. All thinking Americans understand that BHO's intention is to pay off his environmentalist supporters and to further advance his socialist big-government agenda. I'm afraid it's really that simple.

It's going to be a rough four years, folks. What's so stunningly obvious is that our economic and energy problems can be more cost-effectively resolved by the private sector. Big government spending and ill-conceived regulation, historically the single most insidious impediments to a country's economic well-being, will accomplish precious little--but at a staggering cost--to resolve our energy and other economic and security issues. Our political leaders' re-learning this age-old lesson is going to be painful for us all. And, tragically, it's so utterly avoidable.

Man-made climate warming is an unmitigated politically inspired scam, and we'd best see the light soon, or we're all going to be in the dark. Literally.

("In a time of universal deceit, telling the truth becomes a revolutionary act." George Orwell)

("A wise and frugal government, which shall leave men free to regulate their own pursuits of industry and improvement, and shall not take from the worth of labor and bread it has earned--this is the sum of good government." Thomas Jefferson)

Leftist Bullies & America's Future (5/2016)

Amidst the presidential campaign maelstrom, the relentless Progressive violations of our liberties, traditional values, religious freedom, free enterprise, and constitutional underpinnings continue. Now this:

Until I recently read about the 16 Attorneys General--all Progressives, of course--who are promising to target any company that challenges Liberalism's climate change RELIGION, I honestly thought I was beyond being shocked by the Left's propensity for tyranny and bullying.

Reminiscent of the excesses of the Spanish Inquisition of 1478, these fascist high priests intend to vigorously pursue corporate "climate change deniers" to the "fullest extent of the law"--whatever contrived law that might be.

Asserting that "climate change deniers" are committing "fraud" and are, therefore, unprotected by that pesky First Amendment, these modern-day inquisitors--New York State's AG Schneiderman being among them--plan to impose huge fines against anyone who declines to blindly submit to their scientifically unproven man-made global warming religious dogma. ("I am the Lord thy God; thou shalt have no other gods before me." Schneiderman and his co-collaborators have clearly forgotten this divine admonition.)

This undisguised attempt to stifle core political speech and vigorous SCIENTIFIC debate should be roundly condemned by all Americans! AG Schneiderman, among other inquisitors, should not only apologize for his loathsome thuggery; he should either resign or be removed from office.

Is it any wonder the citizens of this deeply divided country are in the throes of despair, uncertainty and anger? Is it any wonder that desperate Americans are turning to "outsiders" like Donald Trump? Is it any wonder that secessionist movements, most notably the Texas Nationalist Movement, are gaining in strength, support and determination?

Make no mistake, folks. Our Founders would NEVER EVER have tolerated the tyranny which now assails us at every turn and from every direction. To a man, they would have full-throatedly counseled civil disobedience, State nullification and, if all else fails, either secession or outright rebellion.

And this: NOTHING--absolutely NOTHING--the British did to Americans in the 18th century which convinced American colonists to secede from England can in any way compare to the awful intensity of today's Progressive assault on our unalienable rights to life, liberty and the pursuit of happiness. And in this terrible light, is it really a stretch to reasonably suggest that this union of sovereign States (as originally conceived anyway) has, in fact, finally outlived its usefulness. (Personally, I believe that our societal, political and economic problems are now so severe and so embedded as to be effectively irremediable. No Pollyanna I.)

So, we can either continue to submit to or otherwise accommodate the intolerable, or we can exercise our unalienable rights to appropriately resist. In any event, I urge all patriots to look solemnly to our Founders for wisdom and direction in these extremely troubling times. And remember this: **unalienable rights are unalienable only to the extent we are determined to defend them.**

("The chasm between conservatives and liberals grows wider by the day. We live in a house divided. This profound difference between people on the Right and Left will have to be managed with diligence if our country is not to fragment and fall apart. Great leadership will be required. This, not income inequality, is the moral issue of our time." Ed Klein, Writer/Reporter, 2015*)*

("Given that the rise of Sanders theatens to extirpate the last vestiges of classical liberalism in the Democratic Party, there has never been a time in my life when limited and accountable government in the United States is under greater threat...classical liberalism will continue to decline." John O. McGinnis, Writer and Professor of Constitutional Law, Northwestern University, 2016*)*

("...any people, anywhere, being inclined and having the power, have the right to rise up and shake off the existing government, and form a new one that suits them better." Congressman Abraham Lincoln on the floor of Congress, 1847*)*

("Whenever the people shall grow weary of the existing government, they can exercise their constitutional right of amending it or their revolutionary right to dismember or overthrow it." Pres. Abraham Lincoln, Inaugural Address, 1861*)*

[10] THE IMMIGRATION HUSTLE

Feds Usurp State Immigration Authority

Being an 'ole immigration counselor, and having perfunctorily accepted the general notion that the feds are, in fact, preeminent in the area of immigration, I decided to research the matter for myself.

Lesson learned yet again: ALWAYS question the feds ANY TIME they claim primacy. Why? Chances are better than even they've overstepped their Art 1 Sec 8 enumerated powers. And, indeed, on the matter of immigration law they have grossly violated the constitution with impunity, proving once again that all the feds require in order to expand their powers are submissive States and an uninformed, disengaged citizenry.

My research into this subject quickly and manifestly shows that federal primacy relates only to matters of *naturalization*, but that *immigration* still remains very much a State power.

We must remember that the Ninth and Tenth Amendments to the Constitution clearly reserve those powers and rights not specifically granted by the Constitution to the federal government to the sovereign States or to the people. Simply put, if a power is not specifically granted to the federal government (Art 1 Sec 8), that power falls within the sole purview of the States. The Ninth was intended to preserve all rights existing under state laws as of 1791. The intention of the Tenth was to prevent future federal encroachments upon the states via its exercise of non-delegated powers.

As the federalistblog points out, "because the States retained just about everything they had before joining the union, and the fact this is clearly enumerated in the Constitution, gives Congress no more authority to authorize entry of immigrants or asylum seekers within the individual States any more than it has the authority to direct another country to accept them."

In fact, before and after the 14th Amendment, most States actually had their own immigration commissioners to supervise state immigration activities as well as state immigration representatives in various foreign countries to encourage legal entries into their states of specially qualified persons. But, by slow erosion of the Constitution over the years, the feds have pretty much usurped nearly all authority over immigration matters. Willfully negligent or otherwise financially dependent, aka bought-off, States have, by their silence over the years, stupidly and irresponsibly consented to this--and countless other--federal encroachments.

Rep. John Bingham, co-author of the14[th] Amendment, argued that while States may not deny entry of US Citizens, States may forbid entry of aliens and to deny their right to acquire property in the States. Surely, 'ole John must have been a crackpot. Huh?

Justice Taney argued Congress has no right to authorize the introduction of aliens without the express consent of the States involved. He also cited Holmes v Jenison, Groves v Slaughter, and Prigg v Pennsylvania to demonstrate that the States alone had the power to expel and exclude. Taney must be another one of those Constitution-first troublemakers!!!

In a note to Congress, Pres. Grant asserted that the federal government was prohibited from interfering with immigration matters and that "responsibility over immigration can only belong with the States since this is where the Constitution kept the power." And all this time I thought Ulysses S. Grant was a nice, upstanding guy!!!

The challenge for the feds over the years has been to prove that immigration somehow directly relates to foreign affairs, thus incident to its exercise of delegated powers under Art 1 Sec 8. However, because the federal government has been unable to constitutionally or cogently demonstrate that relationship, it has simply usurped state authority. And, as said, up to now States have routinely submitted.

While Art 1 Sec 8 specifically grants Congress the power "to establish a uniform Rule of Naturalization, and uniform Laws on the subject of Bankruptcies throughout the United States", nowhere in the Constitution is Congress granted authority over matters related to immigration. NOWHERE!!! (Note: by definition, "immigration" relates to the movement of people while "uniform rules of naturalization" relate solely to citizenship requirements.) Again, the Constitution's enumerated federal powers say absolutely nothing about immigration; thus, if immigration/asylum authority is not expressly granted to the federal government, it is, therefore, expressly withheld from it. (Note: the only allusion to *immigration*, per se, is Art 1 Sec 9 which prohibits the "migration and importation" of slaves after 1808, a deal which the States agreed to as a condition of ratification.)

In a nutshell, for the feds to rightly claim constitutional primacy in immigration--or in any other matter--two conditions must be met: 1) that power must be expressly delegated to the feds, or be "incidental to a delegated power granted to Congress", and 2) that power must be expressly withheld from the States. On this subject, the Constitution very clearly places primacy with the States. But, constitutional primacy is utterly irrelevant if the several States are inclined to ignore or otherwise duck that primacy.

None other than Thomas Jefferson unequivocally stated that States retained jurisdiction and authority over immigration matters: "Alien friends {as opposed to enemy aliens] are under the jurisdiction and protection of the laws of the state within they are; that power over them has been delegated to the United States, nor prohibited to the individual states, distinct from their power over citizens..."

James Madison succinctly explained that "the powers delegated by the proposed Constitution to the Federal Government are few and defined. Those which are to remain in the State governments are numerous and indefinite. The former will be exercised principally on external objects, as war, peace, negotiation, and foreign commerce with which the power of taxation will, for the most part, be connected. The powers reserved to the several States will extend to all the objects, which, in the ordinary course of affairs, concern the lives, liberties, and properties of the people, and the internal order, improvement, and prosperity of the State."

The short of it is this: since the Articles of Confederation, the sovereign States--not the feds--have had exclusive authority over immigration matters, and that authority was carried over into the Constitution itself. Clearly, the culprits here are the States themselves who have cavalierly and gratuitously surrendered their sovereignty.

However, to checkmate further federal violations of the Constitution and to reverse the litany of violations already committed, I urge all readers to do their own research on this and a whole host of other Constitution-related subjects. You may be surprised and very much appalled by the extent of federal overreach perpetrated on the "Republic" over the years. In short, take nothing for granted. Accept nothing at face value. Challenge long-held assumptions, court rulings and popularly held notions about the Constitution which simply don't square with original meaning and clear intent. Don't expect to be properly educated by the media's agenda-driven talking heads and political elites, most of whom have already bought into the myth of federal supremacy in nearly all spheres of our lives. Don't routinely acquiesce to your own State's shortsighted failure to properly assert its constitutional powers.

Finally, on ALL constitutional matters scrupulously question with boldness and probity. Leave no stone unturned. As the final arbiters of what is and what is not constitutional, it is incumbent upon We the People--not a gaggle of dopey self-serving attorneys--to be the experts. Research!!!! To determine what is and what is not constitutional, rely on the Founders, your own integrity, resourcefulness and objectivity, and most certainly NOT on the feds--and not even on your own lackadaisical State authorities who, by their own negligence, have conspired to cede so many of our rights to an increasingly unbridled national government.

Refugees, Politics & Lawlessness (7/2014)

Is Obama preparing to yet again play to his far left globalist base of radical Mexican-American open-border nationalists (*La Raza* quickly comes to mind) by circumventing US immigration law and, of course, Congress? Is there anything this guy won't do to satiate his verminous allies on the Left? That's rhetorical, of course.

Reportedly, Obama is planning to grant refugee status--on a "pilot project" basis, of course--to persons still residing in Nicaragua, El Salvador and Honduras, this to eliminate the threats posed to them should they opt to tackle that long, arduous and dangerous journey through the Mexican heartland in order to illegally breach our southwestern border. How very compassionate. But, isn't that just another way of aiding and abetting gate-crashers? But, no matter. After all, we're talking about poor, innocent suffering children mired in poverty. Right? Surely, we should protect these "refugees" yearning to be free. No?

Just so we're clear as to what the legal definition of *refugee* really is, this: Sec 101(a)(42) of the Immigration & Nationality Act defines a refugee as a person who has fled his/her country of origin owing to a *well-founded fear (clear/reasonable probability) of persecution (threat to life or freedom) on account of race, religion, nationality, membership in a particular social group, or political opinion, and who is unable or unwilling to return to his/her country of origin and to avail himself or herself of its protection.* (Carefully note: if a person still within his/her country of origin, refugee status may be granted on a case-by-case basis by the President, but only AFTER consultation with Congress AND only if that person meets the definition of a refugee.)

As can be seen, there is nothing in this definition which suggests that sub-standard housing, poor diet, poverty, gang wars, or drug cartel shoot-outs are bases for a "well-founded fear of persecution". If that were the case, many folks in Detroit, Chicago and other inner city areas of the US would meet that definition--to say nothing of the nearly billion other people around the world--who would then be within their rights to seek refugee status in the United States!

Excepted from consideration are those who have participated in the persecution of others, who have been convicted of a serious nonpolitical crime or are considered security threats (terrorist activities/ties) to the US.

Normally, a person who has fled his country of origin must first be interviewed by the UN High Commission for Refugees (UNHCR) to determine if, in fact, he/she meets the internationally-accepted definition of a *refugee*, which is essentially that definition already adopted by the US. He/She then falls under the temporary protection of the UN (refugee camp) until such time that a third country agrees to resettle him/her as a refugee or until such time that he/she may be safely repatriated to his/her country of origin, whichever comes first. Resettlement by a third country is conditioned on that third country's having also interviewed him/her to determine if, in fact, s/he does meet the definition of refugee.

As for a person already in the US, per 208(a)(b)(1), *asylee* status may be granted within one year after his/her entry if he/she can demonstrate that, in effect, he/she meets the definition of a refugee. Thus, the only difference between an *asylee* and a *refugee* is that the former is already in the US.

Then, of course, per 212(d)(5), a person, of "significant public interest", may also be *paroled* into the US owing to "urgent humanitarian" or "emergency reasons", e.g. Indochinese during the aftermath of the Vietnam war and Cuban-Haitians.

Let's hope Obama and his political advisors carefully focus on these definitions and requirements before unilaterally committing their political fortunes and our dangerously dwindling wealth to yet another questionable or unlawful way for future voters from Central America to enter the US.

Finally, like their Liberal acolytes, this Administration continues to muddy the waters with political correctness and agenda-driven word-smithing. They deliberately muddle immigration terminology to legitimize the illegitimate. To wit, the term "illegal immigrant" is an oxymoron. By definition, an *immigrant* is a legal entrant--not illegal. An entrant is either an illegal alien/undocumented alien (entered without inspection and US approval) or an immigrant/refugee/asylee/parolee/non-immigrant visa holder. Thus, any person entering our country without inspection/approval enters illegally. By LAW, therefore, that person is an illegal entrant/illegal alien/undocumented alien--NOT an "illegal immigrant"! Within the annals of immigration law there is no such thing as an "illegal immigrant". That term of art is a Liberal contrivance to confound and obfuscate.

Please keep all this in mind when listening to the politically-driven or wholly uneducated cacaphony of chatter in the media. Some is deliberately disinformational. Some is just plain dumb.

Catharsis Alert: Immigrant vs Illegal Alien

This week, Justice Sonia Sotomayor said she was "insulted" that "illegal immigrant" was equated to criminality.

Well, that quickly brought my blood to a bubbly boil, and convinced me that now is as good a time as any to finally get this off my chest by bringing a modicum of clarity to this scramble of immigration terms--not only for Sonia, but everyone else as well. So, here goes...

A retired Associate Director for Immigration and Refugee Services, and a USCIS board-certified Immigration Counselor for 22 years, from the beginning of the open-borders debate I've been both vexed and annoyed by the widespread muddling of the textbook meaning of the term *immigrant*.

For the most part, I have concluded that this muddling has been intentional and has been perpetuated by the Left for the sole purpose of advancing its open-border political agenda. Objectively, there is no other reasonable explanation.

Not surprisingly, the MSM and many clueless folks on the Right as well have either deliberately or unwittingly adopted the paradoxical and misleading use of the term "illegal immigrant" which both adds to the confusion and serves to unfairly legitimize the status of an "illegal alien", aka "undocumented alien", or to de-legitimize the status of immigrants.

The short of it is this: by definition, an immigrant is a legal entrant. He or she was properly inspected and entered the country legally; thus, from a legal standpoint, describing a person as an "illegal immigrant" is self-contradictory for it erroneously describes an immigrant as illegal. To be clear, an entrant is either legal or illegal, i.e. an illegal alien/ undocumented alien OR an immigrant. It is impossible to be both illegal AND an immigrant.

FYI: Those formally granted refugee or asylee status, a non-immigrant visa (tourist, working, etc), or immigrant status (family reunification case) are, of course, legal entrants. They were inspected by US authorities (i.e. documented), granted that legal status and permitted to enter the country legally. And only if a refugee, asylee, non-immigrant (visa holder) or immigrant violates the terms of his/her admission, e.g. overstaying one's visa or committing a serious crime, will his/her status revert to that of illegal/removable/deportable.

And this: from a sociological--not legal--standpoint, all persons who enter the country may be correctly described as "migrants" or, loosely, as "immigrants". But, just as all citizens are not natural-born citizens, not all migrants/immigrants are legal entrants.

Obviously, the use of term "illegal immigrant" merely adds a patina of legitimacy to an illegal alien's/illegal entrant's/undocumented alien's status. And, of course, that is the tendentious political purpose of many dishonest political hacks and word police on the Left, many of whom should know better.

So, please keep this differentiation in mind the next time you hear someone using the asinine term "illegal immigrant". Call 'em on it.

We are a proud nation of **immigrants**--NOT illegal aliens, overs-stayers, undocumented aliens, illegal entrants. Pass it on!

And for the insulted and woefully misinformed Justice Sotomayor, you have the following immigration descriptors to rely upon to define an entrant into the United States: either an illegal alien, undocumented alien, illegal entrant OR legal entrant, legal non-immigrant, immigrant. Confusingly mixing and matching to accommodate your "feelings" or political predisposition is irresponsible, ignorant and shamelessly self-serving. Of more importance, it badly depreciates your credibility as a Supreme Court Justice.

There! That's it. Gee, I'm feeling better already...

Illegal Entry is a Misdemeanor; Illegal RE-Entry is a Felony

During an interview with Bill O'Reilly on August 6th regarding the off-duty border patrol agent who was murdered by two illegal aliens, and much to O'Reilly's astonishment, Lou Dobbs reported that an illegal RE-entry by an illegal alien is a criminal offense. Mr. Dobbs actually cited Section 1325 of the US immigration law to support his claim

It's always a source of elation for me when the heavily opinionated chatter on the various "news" channels is sometimes interrupted by actual facts and a little education. And for that, I am especially grateful to Mr. Dobbs.

Being an 'ole immigration worker in my pre-retirement life, I knew Mr. Dobbs was correct, but, for my own benefit and knowing how immigration law is nearly always in flux, I decided to double-check the accuracy of his report. So, in a nutshell, and for those of you who care, these cites:

--Under **INA Sec 212(a)(9)(C)**, a person who was removed from the US and then tries to enter without going through the required admission procedures will be *permanently barred* from any future entry into the US.

--**Title 8 Section 1325 of the US Code** renders illegal entry a *misdemeanor* carrying with it imprisonment for 6 months for the first offense, and a *felony* and 2 years in prison for the second offense. In short, any alien who (1) enters or attempts to enter at any time or place other than as designated by immigration officials, OR (2) eludes examination or inspection by immigration officers, OR (3) attempts to enter or obtains entry by a willfully false or misleading representation or the willful concealment of a material fact shall, for the first offense, be fined ($50-$250) or imprisoned for not more than 6 months, or both, and, for a subsequent commission of any such offense (illegal re-entry), be fined or imprisoned for not more than 2 years.

I'll bet dollars to donuts this law is very rarely enforced and, for the most part, utterly ignored by the Administration and their open-borders lackeys and supporters.

Just so there's no wiggle room on how one might interpret the meaning of this section of the law, illegal re-entry means one of the following has occurred: alien was (1) denied admission to the US, (2) excluded from the US, (3) deported from the US, (4) removed from the US, or (5) departed the US while an order of exclusion, deportation or removal was outstanding.

With particular respect to the two illegals who murdered the off-duty border patrol agent earlier this week, aliens re-entering or found in the US without government approval, after a criminal conviction for an aggravated felony--which will surely apply in this case--the maximum term of imprisonment is 20 years and a permanent bar from any future entry into the US.

(Note: if an alien illegally re-enters, after a criminal felony conviction for a non-aggravated felony, or after 3 or more misdemeanor convictions for drug-related crimes or crimes against persons, he or she is subject to a fine or imprisonment for up to 10 years, or both.)

Again, thank you, Mr. Dobbs. The education, a rare treat offered up by "news" shows these days, was sincerely appreciated.

AFTERWORD

Did our Founders foresee our Republic's demise or dissolution? In a word, unequivocally.

When in 1787 Dr. Benjamin Franklin stepped outside Independence Hall in Philadelphia, wherein delegates from the various States had fashioned our Constitution, he was met by a woman who eagerly asked if we had a monarchy or a Republic, to which Dr. Franklin famously replied, "You have a Republic, madam, if you can keep it." And as it turns out, keeping our Republic has been a very tall order-- indeed, an abject failure.

From that point forward, our Republic's unraveling began for all the reasons our Founders had wisely anticipated.

Today, in what conservative Mark Levin has insightfully characterized as America's "post-constitutional period", it should be both sobering and, indeed, alarming to realize that 3/4 of our federal laws have been promulgated, not by our elected representatives, but by a faceless, heavy-handed and essentially unaccountable bureaucracy, effectively supplanting bedrock republican principles of governance with imperious bureaucratic rule.

Alien ideology, self-serving party politics, cynical political pandering, a destructive squandering of our national wealth to provide bread and circuses to nurture dependency, the dumbing down of a politically correct population, relentless attempts to legitimize immoral behavior, a calculated effort to destroy our religious foundations and the traditional nuclear family, and widespread ignorance of or hostility toward our foundational constitutional principles, have conspired to bring this country to a tipping point of economic collapse and political suicide.

Astute historians and students of human behavior, the Founders well-understood and apprehended the age-old tendency of human nature to corrupt the best laid and loftiest plans of man. Below is but a sampling of some very astute observations and warnings offered up by our Founders and other historical figures which should give us all pause:

"I agree to the Constitution...and I believe, further, that this is likely to be well administered for <u>a course of years</u>, and can only end in despotism, as other forms have done before it, when the people shall become so corrupted as to need despotic government, being incapable of any other." Benjamin Franklin

"Our Constitution was made only for a moral and religious people. It is wholly inadequate to the government of any other." John Adams

"Our government is now taking so steady a course as to show by what road it will pass to destruction, to wit, by consolidation first, and then corruption... The engine of consolidation will be the federal judiciary; the two other branches the corrupting instruments." Thomas Jefferson

"The spirit of encroachment tends to consolidate the powers of all the departments in one, and thus to create...a real despotism." George Washington

"If Congress can employ money indefinitely, for the general welfare, and are the sole and supreme judges of the general welfare, they may take the care of religion into their hands; they may appoint teachers in every State, county, municipality...and pay them out of the public treasury; they may assume the provision of the poor...Were the power of Congress to be established in the latitude contended for, it would subvert the very foundations, and transmute the very nature of the limited government establishment by the people of America." James Madison

"If destruction be our lot, we must ourselves be its author and finisher. As a nation of freeman, we must live through all time or die by suicide." A. Lincoln

"The will of man is not shattered, but softened, bent, and guided--men are seldom forced by it to act, but they are constantly restrained from acting. Such a power does not destroy, but it prevents existence; it does not tyrannize, but it compresses, enervates, extinguishes, and stupefies a people, till the nation is

reduced to be nothing better than a flock of timid and industrious animals, of which government is the shepherd." Alexis De Tocqueville, Democracy in America, 1830

Do we accept the awful reality of our situation and soberly prepare for peaceful and orderly dissolution, or do we, at our own peril, accommodate and embrace the Godless Progressive agenda and their authoritarian reordering of our lives? This is the critical question before us.

And when you hear Progressives proclaim the virtues of democracy over and over again, remember these sinister quotes:

"Democracy is the road to Socialism": Karl Marx

"Socialism is the road to Communism." Vladimir Ilyich Lenin

Got it?

In the throes of wishful thinking, complacency, confusion, fear, anxiety, anger and uncertainty, with one voice patriots have yet to define a clear remedial course of action going forward. But, time is running out, and seizing upon a practicable remedy to our political and economic miasma cannot be far off.

Faced with the looming threat of political oppression and economic self-destruction, whatever form that remedial course of action may take let us always rely on the wise counsel of our Founders.

Let us never surrender to the utopian assault. In the end, bullies are bullies, and always back down. Standing up in unity to these soulless creatures must be our sacred mission.

"Never give in—never, never, never, never, in nothing great or small, large or petty, never give in except to convictions of honour and good sense. Never yield to force, never yield to the apparently overwhelming might of the enemy." Winston Churchill

ABOUT THE AUTHOR

Jim Delaney, a native of Oneonta and Rochester, NY, earned a Bachelor's Degree in Political Science/International Relations in 1966; after commissioning, he served at the Special Warfare Center/Ft. Bragg as Intelligence Officer for the 92nd Battalion, 2nd Psychological Operations Group; an Infantry Captain, he served in Vietnam and again served at the Special Warfare Center as Chief, Requirements Branch, US Army Institute for Military Assistance. While in military service, he earned the combat infantry badge and two bronze stars for meritorious service and heroism. As a civilian, he served variously as Program Assistant, Field Coordinator or Country Program Director for Catholic Relief Services-USCCB conducting humanitarian, disaster relief and micro-development programs in Asia and Africa. Until his retirement in 2003, he served as Associate Director for Refugee & Immigration Services for the Diocese of Rochester, NY and was a program consultant and trainer in the areas of refugee resettlement and volunteer management until 2006. He is currently a small businessman. Once a member of the Greece and Monroe County Republican Committees, he is now a member of the Conservative Party, the Rochester Tea Party, American Legion, the 912 Group, MOAA, Vietnam Veterans of America, Tenth Amendment Center, NRA, TNM, WTP-NY and GOA. He writes on his own *Opinerlog.blogspot.com* and other conservative sites, and is currently working on another book.